50 Ways to Teach Social Studies for Elementary Teachers

50 Ways to Teach Social Studies for Elementary Teachers

S. Kay Gandy

ROWMAN & LITTLEFIELD
Lanham • Boulder • New York • London

Published by Rowman & Littlefield
An imprint of The Rowman & Littlefield Publishing Group, Inc.
4501 Forbes Boulevard, Suite 200, Lanham, Maryland 20706
www.rowman.com

6 Tinworth Street, London SE11 5AL, United Kingdom

British Library Cataloguing in Publication Information Available

Library of Congress Cataloging-in-Publication Data

Names: Gandy, S. Kay, 1954- author.
Title: 50 ways to teach social studies for elementary teachers / S. Kay Gandy.
Other titles: Fifty ways to teach social studies for elementary teachers
Description: Lanham, Maryland: Rowman & Littlefield, 2021. | Includes bibliographical
    references.
Identifiers: LCCN 2021009207 (print) | LCCN 2021009208 (ebook) |
    ISBN 9781475860689 (cloth) | ISBN 9781475860696 (paperback) |
    ISBN 9781475860702 (epub)
Subjects: LCSH: Social sciences—Study and teaching (Elementary)
Classification: LCC LB1584 .G33 2021 (print) | LCC LB1584 (ebook) |
    DDC 372.83/044—dc23
LC record available at https://lccn.loc.gov/2021009207
LC ebook record available at https://lccn.loc.gov/2021009208

♾️™ The paper used in this publication meets the minimum requirements of American
National Standard for Information Sciences—Permanence of Paper for Printed Library
Materials, ANSI/NISO Z39.48-1992.

Contents

Preface

Teachers have long been known as scavengers and recyclers. We save empty boxes, cans, and tubes and scour the rummage sales and flea markets. An empty oatmeal box can become a drum for a Native American tribe or a telescope for constellations; a cardboard tube can become the base of a rocket or a totem pole; a milk carton can become a house in the community or a planter for seeds. Teachers look for items that can be acquired at little or no cost.

As a former elementary teacher in a poor, rural parish in Louisiana, I have experienced the need to scrounge for resources. The school where I taught for many years had no buses, so most students walked to school. The school had a 98 percent free lunch population and my students often did not have the money to buy school supplies. Each teacher got three reams of paper to last for the year and we did not have a school library, art teacher, physical education, or music teacher. The school was built to hold 400 students, yet our population was 850. Classes met on the stage or wherever a space could be found.

No funds were available from my school district to buy social studies materials. I taught at a Title 1 school, so funds were available to buy some math or reading materials. Even today in many schools there is very little funding available to purchase social studies materials. Over my forty-four years of teaching I have become an expert at teaching on a shoestring budget. Drawing from my own experiences and ideas from many other thrifty teachers, I offer to the reader a variety of suggestions and ideas for the economically challenged classroom.

There are many teachers who spend several hundred dollars of their own money to purchase materials for their classroom or students. I know because I was one of them. With many school districts facing budget constraints, it is good to know that there are a lot of inexpensive resources available to teachers. With all the planning teachers must do and the lack of materials readily available, I believe that teachers will appreciate having a book of ideas to teach social studies with engaging and interesting topics. This book is dedicated to all the teachers who give with their hearts and souls (and money) to the profession. I hope you find the ideas useful and create students who have a lifelong love for learning.

I do need to thank my illustrator, Madalyn Stack. She drew the illustrations and book cover for this book and my previous book *Mapping Is Elementary, My Dear*. I only described the vague ideas in my head for illustrations, and Madalyn quickly put to paper exactly what I needed. It was through her illustrations that I was able to make a secret tribute to my mom in the first book and my teacher friends in this book.

Introduction

Deciding when, what, and how to teach social studies can be dependent upon principals, teachers, state standards, or other external influences. More and more, assessment on social studies content is externally mandated and often limited to certain grade levels. Yet, all teachers are held accountable to teach state social studies standards. Many teachers may believe that following the textbook is the best way to cover all the necessary content in order to meet state curricula, while others search for inspiration outside the norm. Often, textbooks are out of date and there is no funding available to purchase new editions. Whether there is autonomy or total control, it is the students who ultimately benefit or not in the classroom. Teachers providing high-quality education use multiple strategies which increase student knowledge and skills.

For those teachers searching for ideas to teach social studies in fun and meaningful ways, this book provides a plethora of ideas for practical lessons connected to real-world topics and will save the busy teacher time and effort. The fifty activities in this book are housed under themes and include content connections (civics, history, geography, economics), guiding questions, and literacy connections. Guiding questions create a bridge to higher level thinking and help set the purpose for teaching and learning. The literacy connections provide examples of children's literature to accompany each activity, a more engaging source for students as compared to the dull narrative typical in social studies textbooks. Within the activities are suggestions for teaching both older and younger elementary students.

1

Chapter 1 describes how to use primary sources to teach social studies through such artifacts as Petitions for Citizenship, stamps, flea markets, and money. Primary sources are the backbone of teaching social studies. Chapter 2 focuses on the use of music to teach social studies by examining instruments, storytelling, dance, work songs, and nonlinguistic representations. Music is intertwined in daily social life from learning ABC songs, to the use of fight songs at football games, to the use of a particular song at a wedding. Chapter 3 illustrates the use of literature to teach social studies through newspapers, telephone books, poetry, folktales, and origin stories. Using literature helps meet state standards that mandate the use of informational text to learn social studies content. Chapter 4 explores the use of visual images to teach social studies with photographs, cartoons, comics, and movies. Children are visual by nature and will appreciate using visual media to learn social studies.

Chapter 5 focuses on using the environment to teach social studies by examining trail systems, trash, endangered species, land management, and habitats. Using the environment as a starting point to teach social studies concepts connects students to the responsibilities of stewardship and civic life. Chapter 6 introduces the use of communities to teach social studies through main streets, festivals, cemeteries, and iconography. Studying local communities can instill a sense of pride in students. Chapter 7 looks at the use of food to teach social studies through the origin of foods and appliances, recipes and cooking, and literature based around food. Students will enjoy examining similar food types from international cuisines. Chapter 8 explores using experiential activities to teach social studies with mock trials, debates, and simulations. This type of learning allows students to interact, make decisions, and solve problems. The book ends with a summary list of all activities within the chapters.

With the 2013 publication of the C3 Framework (college, career, civic life) by the National Council for Social Studies, states began to revise their social studies standards requirements. Teachers are often perplexed as to how to teach the new standards and are desperate for resources. The goal of this book is to provide fifty engaging activities to give the busy elementary teacher an opportunity to scan for quick lesson ideas.

Chapter 1

Using Primary Sources to Teach Social Studies

Primary sources, such as an autobiography, memoir, oral history, photograph, diary, speech, letter, news film footage, art, newspapers, speeches, documents printed by government agencies, or pottery, provide firsthand testimonies or direct evidence created by witnesses who experienced the events. These artifacts are original records created at the time or soon after events occurred in history. Secondary sources, such as a textbook, magazine article, or commentary, interpret and analyze primary sources.

It is important that students are exposed to multiple perspectives of events that happened in the past. Through the use of primary sources, teachers can engage students in critical thinking questions and have them develop reasoned inferences, explanations, or interpretations of issues and events from the past (or present).[1] Often, the sources can offer insight, challenge biases or stereotypes, encourage empathy, present contradictions, or pose alternative explanations. Students are inserted to the time period they are studying and able to experience life events from the view of a variety of sources. Fortunately for teachers with limited budgets, the National Archives (https://www.archives.gov/) and the Library of Congress (https://www.loc.gov/collections/) have millions of primary sources available online. In addition, these websites have materials to use with students for analyzing primary sources.

The National Archives has analysis worksheets for photographs, artifacts, posters, maps, cartoons, videos, sound recordings, written documents, and artwork. For example, to analyze a written document, students might ask the following questions:

- Are there any special markings on the document?
- Who wrote the document?
- Are there any words you don't know? Look up the definitions.
- When was the document written?
- Why do you think the document was written? Who was the document intended for?
- What is the main idea of the document?
- What is another type of primary resource that might agree or disagree with this document?[2]

It is important that students are able to determine the reliability of resources, particularly in this age when information can be posted on the Internet by anyone, whether accurate or not. Primary sources are fundamental to studying social studies, yet social studies is typically taught through secondary sources. However, primary sources can be challenging to use, as they are sometimes fragmented or difficult to interpret. Obsolete word meanings and social context may hinder student understanding. Eyewitnesses may distort or misinterpret events, sometimes for their own gain. A report may be censored or altered for propaganda. Occasionally, there may exist forged documents that claim to be primary sources. The teacher needs to secure documents from reliable depositories, such as the National Archives and the Library of Congress, to ensure that students are working with true primary sources.

ACTIVITIES USING PRIMARY SOURCES TO TEACH SOCIAL STUDIES

1. Petitions for Citizenship

Content Connections:

Geography, history, civics, economics

Guiding Questions:

- Why would someone move to a different country?
- Where can we find information on immigrants to our area?

Literature Connections:

Lawlor, Veronica. *I Was Dreaming to Come to America: Memories from Ellis Island Oral History Project.* Northbrook, IL: Scott Foresman. 1999.
Morales, Yuyi. *Dreamers.* New York: Neal Porter Books. 2018.
Say, Allen. *Grandfather's Journey.* Torrance, CA: Sandpiper. 2008.
Woodruff, Elvira. *The Memory Coat.* New York: Scholastic Press. 1999.

Naturalization is the process in which an immigrant can become an American citizen. After living in the United States for five years, an alien could "petition" for citizenship. Many naturalization records can be found in county courts, state archives, or online at the National Archives. Information on the petitions typically include the name of the immigrant, arrival date and port in the United States, port of origin, city and country of birth, local address, occupation, name of wife and number of children, and a brief physical description of the immigrant.

Divide students into pairs, give each pair a different petition for citizenship, and have them answer the following questions based on what they read on each document:

- Describe the physical appearance of the immigrant.
- How, when, and where did the immigrant arrive in America?
- What are some promises the immigrant makes?

- Does the immigrant have a family?
- Where is the immigrant from?
- Why do you suppose the immigrant left his homeland?
- What things do you think the immigrant might miss about his homeland?
- Tell about any family members you have that emigrated from a different country.

Have students write a short story about why they think the immigrant left his country. Discuss their hypotheses. Common reasons for immigration that emerge from the discussions might include escape from war, build a better life, escape from religious persecution, political freedom, or family reunification. Have students find the country of origin and port of entry on a map. Through Petitions for Citizenship, students can hypothesize why immigrants would leave a country, formulate conclusions about success in the new country, and test solutions with their own family history.

For the younger students, introduce stories of real immigrants from the book *I Was Dreaming to Come to America: Memories from Ellis Island Oral History Project* (Lawlor, 1999). Based on the stories, have the students create their own Petitions for Citizenship using a simple form to note name, country of birth, and reasons why they want to become a citizen of the United States. Explain to students that once an immigrant moves to a country they do not automatically become a citizen. Discuss the Statue of Liberty and how it represents the millions of Americans who passed through Ellis Island.

2. What's in Your Wallet?[3]

Content Connections:

History, economics

Guiding Questions:

- What kind of primary documents do people carry in their wallets?
- What do these documents say about what is important to them?

Literature Connections:

Axelrod, Alan. *Lincoln's Last Night: Abraham Lincoln, John Wilkes Booth, and the Last Thirty-Six Hours Before the Assassination.* New York: Chamberlain Brothers. 2005.

Landis, Matthew. *The Not So Boring Letters of Private Nobody*. London: Puffin Books. 2019.

Discuss with students how the items we carry with us in a purse or wallet can say a lot about who we are and what is important to us. Most people carry money, photographs, credit cards, and medical information. Share things from your own wallet. Ask students what things might change in their wallet as they get older.

Investigate the wallet of a famous American, such as Abraham Lincoln.[4] During the investigation of his murder, the contents of Lincoln's pockets and wallet were examined. Items included two pairs of spectacles, lens polisher, pocketknife, watch fob, linen handkerchief, a playbill, a Confederate $5 bill, a copy of the Gettysburg Address, and eight newspaper articles (including several favorable to the president and his policies). Have students examine photographs of each artifact and summarize the details of the artifact. Assign categories to these primary sources, such as social, political, economic, or historical. Encourage students to discuss the following questions:

- Why do you think President Lincoln carried this particular object with him in his wallet?
- What meaning do you think the artifact had for President Lincoln?
- What kinds of artifacts do you think might be in the wallet if we had looked there four years earlier?
- If Abraham Lincoln were president today, what kinds of things might he carry in his wallet?

Ask students to identify the five most important events in their lives and discuss why those events are most significant. What primary- or secondary-source documents might they carry in a purse or wallet to document these events?

For younger students, have them brainstorm ideas of documents that can describe who they are. For example, a picture with your family might prove you are a son or daughter; a chart on the wall might prove you are in Mrs. Jones's first grade class. Take manila folders and cut handles to shape them into a bag/suitcase/purse. Have students draw documents or pictures, or cut out magazine pictures, to show who they are with primary-type documents.

3. Money, Money, Money

Content Connections:

History, civics, economics

Guiding Questions:

- Who decides what symbols are on money and why?
- Why are there so many kinds of currencies in the world?

Literature Connections:

Mollel, Tololwa. *My Rows and Piles of Coins*. Boston: Clarion Books. 2019.
Worth, Bonnie. *One Cent, Two Cents, Old Cent, New Cent: All About Money (Cat in the Hat's Learning Library)*. New York: Random House Books for Young Readers. 2008.

Many archaeological findings have included some type of coin. Typically, coins are made of precious metals, are usually round, and have some sort of seal of authenticity. Coins have been made of copper, bronze, silver, and gold. Early coins honored leaders and gods. Some were stamped with impressions of everyday life. Coins are primary sources that can teach art, architect, economics, government, and religion.

Give each group of students a handful of coins. Ask questions about the coins, such as the following:

- How much is the coin worth?
- What symbols or pictures are on the coin?
- What writing is on the coin? What do the words mean?
- Which coin has the greater value? The least value?
- Which is the largest coin? The smallest coin? Does size relate to value?

Show various types of currency to students. Explain the names of currency and explore their origins: British pound sterling, Japanese yen, Swiss franc, Swedish krona, Indian rupee, or Spanish peso. Have students look at and discuss various symbols of currency: £ (pound), ¥ (yen), € (euro), $ (U.S. dollar). Have students determine the value of each type of currency and the exchange rate with the U.S. dollar. Ask students the following questions: Who decides what is pictured on currency? Are only people featured on currency (the South African rand features the "big five" animals searched for on the game reserves)? Why do you suppose there is not a one world currency? Have students create a new coin and decide its size, shape, and symbols to be stamped on the coin. How much would it be worth? What writing would you put on your coin? Why?

For younger students, collect quarters that represent different states and discuss the specific symbols that represent each state. Tell students that the principal would like for them to design a coin or bill to represent the school. Encourage students to contribute ideas of symbols that could represent the school. Use clay or soft dough and cover with aluminum foil to make coins. Imprint designs with plastic knives.

4. Stamp Your Story[5]

Content Connections:

Geography, history, civics, economics

Guiding Questions:

- How have stamps changed over time?
- What types of events, places, and people are depicted on stamps?

Literature Connections:

Gibbons, Gail. *The Post Office: Mail and How It Moves*. New York: Collins. 1986.

Jonath, Leslie. *Postmark Paris: A Story in Stamps*. San Francisco: Chronicle Books. 2005.

Wright, Jamie E. *Six Snuglets and the Stamp*. North Charleston, SC: Palmetto Publishing Group. 2019.

Stamps provide a wealth of social studies topics through themes, portraits, symbols, commemorations, geography, technology, or culture. In 1840, the very first postage stamp was issued by Britain and featured Queen Victoria. This stamp, known as the Penny Black, had to be cut out with scissors to be used. The first adhesive postage stamps in the United States were the ten cent George Washington and five cent Benjamin Franklin.[6] Stamps are primary sources which honor artists, writers, musicians, inventors, places, holidays, and events. Postage stamps also depict concepts, such as freedom, exploration, war, and community. There have been controversies surrounding commemorative stamps and even historical errors made on stamps. Several pictures on stamps have been upside down, such as the Jenny plane from World War I. This makes a stamp worth more. Some stamps are worth millions of dollars.

Encourage students to sort stamps by themes or research an event or person depicted on the stamp.[7] After viewing various commemorative stamps, have students create their own stamp to celebrate or honor a person or event. Encourage students to explain why they chose this person or event to commemorate. Students can correspond with pen pals and collect stamps from around the world. Introduce students to the term "philatelist," a stamp collector, and start a stamp club. Another stamp activity is to examine how the price of stamps changed over the years. In 2007, the post office issued the "forever" stamps, which stay valid even with a rate increase. Challenge students to decide what the next stamp should commemorate.

For younger students, provide a variety of stamps and have students decide how to classify them: color, event, cost, size, site, art, and so on. Free stamps can be obtained through the American Philatelic Society. Assign students to create a stamp album about themselves. Stamps can represent hobbies, likes, dislikes, friends, pets, vacations, and so on.

5. The Flea Market[8]

Content Connections:

History

Guiding Questions:

• Why is it important to learn from the past?
• At what point is an item labeled to be from the past?

Literature Connections:

Anno, Mitsumasa. *Anno's Flea Market.* New York: Philomel. 1984.
Herrera, Juan. *Grandma and Me at the Flea (Los Meros Meros Ramateros).* New York: Lee & Low Books, Inc. 2013.

Using concrete items in the classroom can stimulate curiosity and activate investigations into history. An item, such as a hornbook (early primer for school children), can motivate classroom discussions and foster critical thinking skills. There are many items that can be bought cheaply at a flea market or collected from family members that would instigate discussions of change over time. For example, show students a buttonhook and ask them how they think it might have been used. Let the students touch the object, draw it, measure it, and weigh it. Discuss the materials used to create the buttonhook. Explain that shoes in the past buttoned instead of tied and the buttonhook was used to facilitate the closing. The hook was also used for gloves and clothing. Talk with students about how shoes were manufactured, what materials were used, and what shoe fashions are outdated.

Encourage students to bring something "old" from home. Have students ask their caregivers about the history of the item and how it should be used. Set up a class museum and invite other students to come by and learn about the various antiques.

Artifacts can be used as a springboard to create a Jackdaw for an era of history. Named after the British bird that adds brightly colored objects to its nest, the Jackdaw is a collection of primary documents (e.g., maps, photos, newspapers, recipes, video, audio recordings) or artifacts. For example, in the civil rights–era Jackdaw, you could include a copy of a painting of Ruby Bridges (the first African American child to integrate a white school in New Orleans) entering the school with federal marshal escorts, a photograph of a lunch counter sit-in, an audio recording of Martin Luther King Jr.'s "I Have a Dream" speech, and a poster proclaiming "Whites Only."

For younger students, you can use artifacts as a "show and tell" session from the past. Dress as a schoolmarm from the 1800s and give various students objects to tell about as if they were living in this time period. It may be fun to let the students tell about the artifacts in their own words without really knowing what they are, then explaining to the class the real uses of the artifacts. Buttons can also be used to introduce students to history. Buttons can be sorted or classified by color, shape, size, and number of holes. Historically, buttons have been decorative, functional, and made from every imaginable material. Some indicated wealth or rank, others are responsible for nicknames. The term "Cops" evolved from "Coppers," which referred to the large copper buttons on police uniforms.[9] A history of button collecting and information on the National Button Society can be found at https://www.nationalbuttonsociety.org/.

6. Primary Debate[10]

Content Connections:

Civics

Guiding Questions:

- Why should primary documents be used in debates?
- Why is it important to listen to other perspectives on an issue?

Literature Connections:

Murguia, Bethanie Deeney. *We Disagree*. San Diego, CA: Beach Lane Books. 2020.

Rosenthal, Amy Krouse and Tom Litchenheld. *Duck! Rabbit!* San Francisco, CA: Chronicle Books, LLC. 2013.

Using the National Archives or the Library of Congress websites find two primary sources that present opposing views of a topic, such as climate change or current immigrant issues. Divide the class in half and have each half read a different document. Then pair each student with someone who read the other document. As the students discuss what they read have them list the issues and opposing views. Note any evidence used to support the varying positions. Assign students a pro or con side and conduct a classroom debate. Encourage students to do further investigations on the controversial topics. A variation of this lesson would be to select several social history topics for students to investigate and find oral histories on these topics. Have students work in small groups to select a topic, then read and discuss the selected documents. Each group would generate five questions they would like to investigate further.

For younger students, read the book *Duck! Rabbit!* (Rosenthal and Litchenheld, 2003) in which two characters debate whether a creature they see is a rabbit or duck. You might also read the poem "The Blind Men and the Elephant" by John Godfrey Saxe (1872). Each of the six men felt a different part of the elephant and described their ideas of what an elephant looks like. Discuss why people might disagree on something and what they should do about it.

7. Tiles and Patterns[11]

Content Connections:

Geography, history

Guiding Questions:

- Why are tiles a sustainable building tool?
- What types of patterns are made with tiles?

Literature Connections:

De Miguel, Berta and Kent Diebolt. *Immigrant Architect: Rafael Guastavino and the American Dream.* Thomaston, ME: Tilbury House Publishers. 2020.

Field, Robert. *Geometric Patterns from Islamic Art and Architecture and How to Draw Them.* United Kingdom: Tarquin Group. 1998.

Field, Robert. *Geometric Patterns from Tile and Brickwork and How to Draw Them.* United Kingdom: Tarquin Group. 1996.

Tiles have a 5,000-year-long history that traverses across Asia, Africa, and Europe. The Chinese produced baked ceramics pottery in ovens. The production of glazed clay tile has been attributed to the Egyptians. It was, however, the Muslim Moors of North Africa who spread the use to Portugal and throughout Europe. During the height of its wealth, Portugal exported tiles to its colonies. Tiles lined vaults, domes, stairways, pools, castles, park benches, monasteries, and even street signs throughout Portugal. Over the years, various themes were portrayed with tile images, from mythological subjects, to landscape themes, to abstract and geometric patterns.

Tile was a popular building tool in tropical climates. The surfaces reflected heat and light, keeping the interiors cool, and were easy and cheap to maintain. Tiles were also water resistant, fighting against mold and mildew. It was a healthy building tool that was sustainable and did not harm the environment.

Tiles are found in subway stations, churches, restrooms, restaurants, houses, and railway stations. Tile buildings are still in existence all over the world. Excavations at Pompeii have revealed painted tiles that are still bright and beautiful. The U.S. Capitol Building has over 1,000 different tile patterns in its corridors.[12]

Students can make their own tile patterns in the classroom using a salt dough recipe found in appendix A. Students can research historical tile patterns at https://www.pinterest.com/wendyeclarke/historical-design/, or create their own patterns. Challenge students to create tiles to represent an event in history, the culture of their school, or a geographic place.

Younger students can create tiles to represent themselves or a family member. To encourage collaboration, pair with the art teacher or parents to help with the project. Tiles can be used to create patterns for math, illustrate cycles in science, represent characters and events from stories, represent modes of transportation, and so on.

8. Can You Dig It?[13]

Content Connections:

Geography, history

Guiding Questions:

- How do archaeologists find significant sites?
- What do archaeologists do?
- Why is the work of an archaeologist important?

Literature Connections:

Baker, Amanda. *Can You Dig It? Archaeology Lost & Found in the Sands of Time*. Independently Published. 2017.

Duke, Kate. *Archaeologists Dig for Clues*. New York: HarperCollins Children's Books. 1996.

Guillain, Charlotte. *The Street Beneath My Feet*. London: Words & Pictures. 2017.

Logan, Claudia. *The 5,000-Year-Old Puzzle: Solving a Mystery of Ancient Egypt*. New York: Farrar, Straus and Giroux. 2002.

Posner, Jackie. *Magic School Bus Shows and Tells: A Book about Archaeology*. New York: Scholastic Inc. 1997.

The fascination with buried treasures and lost civilizations transcends all ages. Connecting students to the past gives them a better understanding of their own present and future. Where else can the study of trash yield significant insights into how people once lived, worked, and played?

The misconception that students may have is that the only role of an archaeologist is to dig up sites. Archaeologists spend a lot of time in laboratories analyzing and classifying artifacts, working in museums, teaching at universities, writing grants to raise money, or publishing in scholarly journals.

Explore with students the ways that archaeological sites have been discovered: aerial reconnaissance, remote sensing, geophysical survey, agricultural practices, construction, and documents from the past. Excavation can occur under the sea, under the ground, and in mounds or monuments. Dig sites are often found by accident as new construction takes place, natural disasters occur, or fields are plowed. Workers digging a well in China found the terra cotta warriors. A boy throwing stones in cave beside the Dead Sea found pots with Dead Sea Scrolls. Students should be aware that some Native American groups oppose excavation. Debate the reasons a group may not want a site disturbed (e.g., status as a sacred ground) versus the importance of studying and understanding the past.

Assign students different subjects to research for a culture: religion, clothing, jewelry, food, beliefs, rituals, communication, survival, leisure, or economy. To show the work of archaeologists, collect small clay pots for each student from a garden store. Tell students that they are members of an ancient civilization noted for its pottery/artistic skills and require each student to paint the pots with symbols that are representative of his or her life. Display the artwork for a week in the classroom. Over the weekend, wrap each pot in a towel and hit the pot once with a hammer. Place the broken pieces in Ziploc bags of potting soil, taking away one piece from each pot and placing it in the bag of another pot. The next time the class meets explain to students that they will become amateur archaeologists that day. Give each student a bag of pottery pieces and explain that they are to use glue to "reconstruct" the clay pots. Students will use the assembled pot to describe characteristics of the culture of the pot-painter.[14]

The type of environment in which artifacts are found determines how well the artifact is preserved. To show students how ice preserves objects, place various items into plastic cups: bread, blueberry, nail, paper clip, leaf, paper. Fill each cup three-fourth's full of water and place them in a freezer. Remove the cups from the freezer after four days and let the ice melt. Remove objects with tweezers and write down the condition of each object. Have any of them changed? Place the objects in a dry, bright place for four days then look at their conditions. How do they look? Although ice is a great preserver, artifacts will not last long if exposed to moisture, heat, and sunlight.[15]

To focus student attention on artifacts and their meanings, have students pretend they have been chosen to select objects to send to a distant place where nothing is known about the United States. The class will eventually decide on twenty artifacts that will portray life in the United States to future archaeologists.

For younger students, ask if dinosaurs and people lived on Earth together? Use three different color cake mixes to create an Earth cake. The bottom layer should contain several plastic dinosaurs, the middle layer should be left bare, and the top layer should contain plastic people. The middle layer is plain because layers of Earth were laid down for millions of years between the time of dinosaurs and the time of humans. Divide the class into groups to excavate the "earth cake," using a grid system to accurately mark each section.[16] A grid system breaks a section of ground (in this case, cake) into small squares for study. Squares are usually marked with rope or string. Dental floss would work well for the cake. The grids should be assigned numbers so that the student archaeologist can note where anything significant is found.

NOTES

1. Laurel R. Singleton and James R. Giese, "Using Online Primary Sources with Students," *The Social Studies* 90, no. 4 (1999): 148–151, DOI: 10.1080/00377999909602406.

2. Adapted from "Analyze a Written Document," National Archives, accessed January 17, 2020, https://www.archives.gov/files/education/lessons/worksheets/written_document_analysis_worksheet_novice.pdf.

3. Adapted from lesson "What's in Your Wallet," NEH Workshop Lincoln and the Forging of America at the Southern Illinois University Edwardsville, July 24, 2008, accessed January 15, 2020, https://www.siue.edu/education/neh/7-12wallet.shtml.

4. Pictures of items from Lincoln's pockets can be found at the Library of Congress website, https://www.loc.gov/item/scsm001049/.

5. Information from S. Kay Gandy and Cynthia Williams Resor, "Changing Technology and the U.S. Mail," *The Social Studies* 103, no 6 (2012): 226–232.

6. "Stamps and Postcards," USPS, accessed January 17, 2020, https://about.usps.com/who-we-are/postal-history/stamps-postcards.htm#history.

7. Joseph M. Kirman and Chris Jackson, "The Use of Postage Stamps to Teach Social Studies Topics," *The Social Studies* 91, no. 4 (2000): 187–190.

8. S. Kay Gandy, "Teaching Social Studies on a Shoestring Budget," *Social Education* 69, no. 2 (2005): 98–101.

9. Zita Thornton, "Buttons," *Antiques & Collecting Magazine* 106, no. 7 (2001): 26–30.

10. Adapted from lesson ideas in Singleton and Giese, "Using Online Primary Sources with Students."

11. Information from S. Kay Gandy, "Azulejos: Tile Buildings in Iquitos," *Journal of Geology & Geosciences* 3, no. 6 (2014), DOI:10.4172/2329-6755.1000176.

12. "Minton Tiles," Architect of the Capitol, accessed August 20, 2020, https://www.aoc.gov/explore-capitol-campus/art/minton-tiles.

13. Information from S. Kay Gandy, "Connections to the Past: Creating Time Detectives with Archaeology," *Social Education* 71, no. 5 (2014): 267–271.

14. Adapted from lesson by Dianne McWilliams and Betty Giroud, teacher consultants with the Louisiana Geography Education Alliance.

15. Richard Panchyk, *Archaeology for Kids: Uncovering the Mysteries of our Past* (Chicago: Chicago Review Press, 2003): 30.

16. Connie Nobles, *Adventures in Classroom Archaeology* (Baton Rouge, LA: Division of Archaeology, 1992): 10–12.

Chapter 2

Using Music to Teach Social Studies

Dr. Tassel

Drill and practice can be mind-numbing for students who learn better through creative modes. As one of Howard Gardner's multiple intelligence areas, music can be used to teach social studies content to students. Music has a powerful appeal to students of all ages and can be used to enhance children's ability to recall information. The pattern and rhythm of songs seem to hold their attention and get them excited about learning. Not only can music be used as a memory device but it can also be used as a primary source for historical background or a secondary source in a creative assignment.[1] Students could analyze word symbols for the Underground Railroad from the song "Follow the Drinking Gourd," or research the history behind the penning of "The Star-Spangled Banner."

Most students listen to some type of music daily, therefore music is a great motivational tool. Parents and teachers have been using music as a teaching tool for years. In the early years at home, toddlers learn their ABCs through the familiar alphabet song, subtraction through the "Five Little Monkeys Jumping on the Bed" song, and body parts through the "Hokey Pokey" song. Music is a part of children's games and daily life.

Music is threaded throughout the daily lives of many people and is often used in work, sports, religion, communication, and even preserving history. There is a shared vocabulary of music and movement that helps provide unity and strength among diverse peoples. Music is used at shopping malls, at social gatherings, in politics, and in ceremonial life. It has a role in healing, with announcements, and at weddings and funerals.

Music can be used in the classroom for a variety of activities:

- Timer for completing activities
- Transitions between activities
- Teaching content
- Brain breaks (quick time for exercise to music)
- Calming background music
- Connections to eras of history
- Broadening cultural horizons of students
- Celebrations of holidays and events
- Introduction to traditions
- Language arts (analyze sayings, "weave a song" or "spin a tale")

Songs like the "Flight of the Bumblebee" (Nikolai Rimsky-Korsakov, 1900) or the Jeopardy game show TV theme (Greg Kihn Band, 1983) can hurry students through a transition or timed event. Chants or raps can teach rhyme, rhythm, or alliteration. Tempos and beats can encourage movement or physical activity. Music can be used to motivate shy learners by having students sing together with a karaoke machine. For students who are not musical, clapping, stomping, snapping, whistling, and humming are great ways to make music. You might share the musical "Stomp" (co-creators Steve McNicholas and Luke Cresswell, 1991), in which everyday objects are turned into percussive instruments.

There are many benefits of using music in the classroom. Children can make music whatever their background or circumstance. There are multiple means for expression and engagement. There is a diversity of musical genres to appeal to every learner. Because music is prevalent at sports events, at weddings, at funerals, at church services, on car radios, and on cell phones, it becomes the voice of the everyday man in social studies.

ACTIVITIES USING MUSIC TO TEACH SOCIAL STUDIES

9. Teaching Concepts through Music

Content Connections:

Geography, history

Guiding Questions:

- How does music connect to a place?
- How is history preserved through music?

Literature Connections:

Barton, Chris. *88 Instruments.* New York: Knopf Books for Young Readers. 2016.

Cox, Judy. *My Family Plays Music.* New York: Holiday House. 2018.

Flint, Katy. *The Story Orchestra: Carnival of the Animals: Press the Note to Hear Saint Saëns' Music.* London: Frances Lincoln Children's Books. 2020.

Grady, Cynthia. *Like a Bird: The Art of the American Slave Song.* Minneapolis, MN: Millbrook Picture Books. 2016.

Lithgow, John. *Never Play Music Right Next to the Zoo.* New York: Simon & Schuster Books for Young Readers. 2013.

One way to make connections to social studies through music is to introduce the music of a particular time period. For example, "The Streets of

Laredo" (Johnny Cash, 1965), "Home on the Range" (Vernon Dalhart, 1927), "Sweet Betsy from Pike" (Harry McClintock, 1932), and "I've Been Working on the Railroad" (Sandhills Sixteen, 1927) depict the era of early American life in the west. Students will research to discover if the songs were work songs or used for entertainment. An online search of musical instruments and Egypt might turn up descriptions of rattles, tambourines, bells, lyres, flutes, and cymbals. Ask students what the instruments were made from, what they were specifically used for, and how they were played.

The culture of a place can readily be discovered through lyrics of popular songs from the area. For example, the song "Jambalaya" (Hank Williams, 1952) provides insight into vocabulary used in the French Triangle of Louisiana: filé gumbo, bayou, crawfish pie, pirot. Challenge students to guess the meaning of words they are unfamiliar with. Then ask students to think about words in their culture that someone from a different area may not be familiar with.

"Jambalaya" was a popular song on the radio, as was another song great for teaching history, "The Battle of New Orleans" (1959) sung by Johnny Horton. This song gives a comical version of what happened at the battle. Require students to research the actual battle and compare to the song version. Then have students rewrite the song to be more accurate.

Students can find songs that connect to the history and geography of their states. For example, in Kentucky, students will find the unique Shaker music sung at the South Union and Pleasant Hill Shaker sites; learn about the movement of Kentuckians to jobs in the north through Dwight Yoakam's "Readin', Rightin', Route 23" (1987); and review Stephen Foster's antislavery ballad, "My Old Kentucky Home" (1853). Encourage students to write their own song about their state.

Students might also enjoy taking popular songs and writing lyrics to share social studies content. An excellent example is "Too Late to Apologize—A Declaration."[2] Soomo Publishing wrote a parody of the original song "Apologize" by OneRepublic that features Thomas Jefferson singing about the Declaration of Independence. Challenge students to write about an event in history or a current event following this example. They can even make their own music video!

Both *Schoolhouse Rock!*, animated musical short films from the 1970s, and *Animaniacs*, an animated comedy series from the 1990s, provide songs that are still timely today and can be found on YouTube to teach social studies content. "The Preamble," "I'm Just a Bill," and "Three Ring Government" from *Schoolhouse Rock!* are favorites to teach about America's government. From *Animaniacs*, "Wakko's America" teaches states and capitals, "The Ballad of Magellan" teaches the voyages of the Portuguese explorer, and "The Presidents Song" describes the first forty-two presidents of the United States.

Music can even be used as an assessment tool for content knowledge. Give each student a map of the United States with no state labeled. Play snippets of songs that mention places and have the students mark the places on the map. Suggested songs include "Pennsylvania Polka," "New York New York," "My Old Kentucky Home," "Oklahoma," and "Georgia on My Mind." If you want to challenge students, use clips of songs that mention specific cities: "Galveston," "Chicago," "Hooray for Hollywood," "Houston," "San Antonio Stroll," and "Only in Miami." You may challenge students to find songs that name the most places, such as "God Bless the USA" and "This Land Is Your Land."

Younger students will enjoy learning social studies content by singing songs created by the teacher to familiar tunes. Take a song, such as "Mary Had a Little Lamb," and substitute words to teach the concepts:

The Ocean Song (tune: "Mary Had a Little Lamb")
I know oceans on the earth, on the earth, on the earth
I know oceans on the earth, and I can name them now
Arctic, Southern, Indian, Atlantic, Pacific
I know oceans on the earth, and I can name them now

The Continent Song (tune: "Mary Had a Little Lamb")
North and South America, Africa, Antarctica
Europe, Asia, Africa, I know the continents

10. Music with a Message

Content Connections:

Civics

Guiding Questions:

- Why do politicians use music with their campaigns?
- How is music used to get a message out to listeners?

Literature Connections:

Kroll, Steven. *By the Dawn's Early Light: The Story of the Star-Spangled Banner.* New York: Scholastic Press. 2000.

Levy, Debbie. *Soldier Song: A True Story of the Civil War.* New York: Little, Brown and Company Books for Young Readers. 2017.

Rustad, Martha E. H. *Can You Sing the Star-Spangled Banner?* Minneapolis, MN: Cloverleaf Books. 2014.

Schubert, Lida. *Listen: How Pete Seeger Got America Singing.* New York: Roaring Book Press. 2017.

Stotts, Stuart. *We Shall Overcome: A Song that Changed the World.* Boston: Clarion Books. 2010.

To integrate music into civics content, students can pretend they are candidates for political offices. Ask students, "What music would you use for your campaign? Why?" Have students research current political candidates to see what music they use in their campaigns. How does music affect the voters?

Ask student to think of any songs today that give a social or political message. Share with students songs that are pro-war—"Over There" by George M. Cohan (1917), "Have You Forgotten" by Darryl Worley (2003), "Soldiers and Jesus" by James Otto (2010)—and anti-war—"I Ain't Marchin' Anymore" by Phil Ochs (1965), "Give Peace a Chance" by John Lennon (1969), "One Tin Soldier" by Original Caste (2005). Students can write their own songs to take a political stance.

For younger students, play the national anthem, "The Star-Spangled Banner." Identify the American flag as the star-spangled banner. Discuss with students the various places that the national anthem is sung: race car events, football games, graduations, military ceremonies, schools. Introduce the idea of how music can be a symbol of a place. Play other types of symbolic music, such as "America the Beautiful" and "My Country, 'Tis of Thee." Ask students to consider what song might represent their classroom. Encourage students as a group to create an anthem that symbolizes their classroom.

11. Nonlinguistic Representations

Content Connections:

Geography, history

Guiding Questions:

- How can visual images represent music?
- How can music represent visual images?

Literature Connections:

Guns N' Roses. *Sweet Child o' Mine*. New York: Jimmy Patterson. 2020.

Guthrie, Woody. *This Land Is Your Land*. New York: Little, Brown Books for Young Readers. 2020.

Nelson, Kadir. *He's Got the Whole World in His Hands*. New York: Dial Books. 2005.

Through the use of nonlinguistic representations, students are able to construct meaning of content through visual images. Graphic organizers, models, pictures, drawing, and kinesthetic activities are powerful tools to help with student learning. Music can be integrated into these tools to teach social studies concepts. Songbooks are especially entertaining for students.

Place students into groups and assign a patriotic song to illustrate, research the author and time period the song was written, and create their own songbooks. Good songs to research are "The Star-Spangled Banner," "Yankee Doodle," and "America the Beautiful." Groups can share their songbook stories and then sing together with the class.

Mobiles and quilts can also be used to illustrate songs. "This Land Is Your Land" by Woody Guthrie (1944) works well with this type of media. Have students create symbols from construction paper to represent content from the song (e.g., state of California, tree for forest, cactus for desert). Tie the symbols onto a coat hanger to form a mobile. For the quilt, students can color scenes from the song on eight-and-a-half by eleven inch pieces of paper and glue onto construction paper. Piece together to make a quilt of the song.

For the younger students, teach about rivers through the song "The River" by Garth Brooks (1992). Talk about the meaning of the words with students (e.g., "choose to chance the rapids and dare to dance that tide"). Ask students to describe what kind of drawing might illustrate these words. Use drawing paper to write lines from the lyrics. Allow each student to draw and color a picture to represent the lines from the song. Put the lyrics in order, create a cover page, and bind the songbook. Sing the song together as you show each page of the songbook.

12. Musical Instruments

Content Connections:

Geography, history, civics

Guiding Questions:

- How might the environment affect the type of musical instrument prevalent in a region?
- How many ways can you make music?
- How might an instrument represent a culture?

Literature Connections:

Andrews, Troy. *Trombone Shorty*. New York: Harry N. Abrams. 2015.
Margarita Engle. *Drum Dream Girl: How One Girl's Courage Changed Music*. Boston: HMH Books for Young Readers. 2015.
Venable, Colleen. *The Oboe Goes Boom Boom Boom*. New York: Greenwillow Books. 2020.

Talk about instruments that may be specific to a state or culture. Do some cultures make their own instruments from materials in the environment? For example, Kentucky's official state instrument is the dulcimer, which was made of wood from a particular area of the mountains where a builder lived. The dulcimer has many nicknames: dulcymore, harmonium, mountain dulcimer, and hog fiddle. In Louisiana, the washboard is an instrument used with zydeco music. Native peoples made leg rattles from turtle shells. Search on YouTube for musical instruments to share the sounds with students. The accordion is an instrument that will be popular in many cultures. Decorate instruments to depict an assigned culture. You might also find music from a culture and play along with the homemade instruments.

Focus on one instrument with students, such as bells. Students are probably familiar with the most famous bell in American history, the Liberty

Bell. Ask students, how have bells been used to signal important events in history? Bells have been used in religious ceremonies, rung during worship or at funerals, tolled hours, warned of attacks, and announced events. Some cultures have used bells to bring rain or disband storms, evoke curses or obstruct demons.[3] Sailors use bells to indicate the end of a watch. Teachers used handheld bells to start the school day. The Bible describes how small bells were worn on the hems of priests' garments. Catholic priests often rang a bell after saying the words of consecration.

Have students look for bell towers (e.g., Big Ben in London, the bell tower at Notre Dame, Campanile di San Marco in Venice, Italy). The original purpose of bell towers was to let the community know of dangerous situations or special events. A sequence of bell tones indicates time on the hour, half hour, and quarter hour. In the eighteenth and nineteenth centuries, bell towers were the public timekeepers. Have the students search their own community or state for bell towers.

Some bells are used as musical instruments. Introduce handbells, chimes, and the carillon to students. Share popular music that uses bells in the music: "Hells Bells" (AC/DC, 1980), "For Whom the Bell Tolls" (Metallica, 1984), "Carol of the Bells" (Nox Arcana, 2005), "Tubular Bells" (Mike Oldfield, 1973), and "Sleigh Ride" (Leroy Anderson, 1959). Assign students various countries to research and find out how bells have been used across the world. Students can investigate the costs of making the bells, the geographic significance of the location of the bells, and the civic uses of the bells.

Drum circles are popular, not as a preparation for a performance but as a means of joining on a group project. It is a tool for celebrating community, life, and unity through rhythm and music. Since most anything can be used as a percussive instrument, it would be easy to host a drum circle with students. No level of expertise is required, and everyone is welcome. Some activities to do in the drum circle include the following:

- repeat back rhythms
- play at different speeds
- beat rhythms to poetry
- improvise rhythms
- "talk" to each other with a beat
- echo each other

- play at different dynamics (loud, soft)
- explore sounds (metal, wood, shakers)
- starting and stopping together

To connect to social studies, teachers can introduce the roots of rhythm, the origin of various percussive instruments, and the importance of drums in various cultures. Drums have been used in religious ceremonies, on the battlefield to terrify enemies, in the field for harvesting purposes, and even as medicinal tools.

For the younger students, discuss how instruments can be made of many different types of materials. Some materials might come from nature (wood, gourds, turtle shells, animal skin). Other materials might be recycled from scrap metal, oil drums, and old cars. A piece of wax paper over a comb can make a homemade kazoo. An empty oatmeal box becomes a drum, or a toilet paper roll filled with beans becomes a maraca. Experiment with your own "instruments at hand." Use easy-to-find materials such as pie pans, beads, spoons, duct tape, plastic eggs, boxes, or cardboard tubes.

Find something in the classroom, or at home, that is not usually considered a musical instrument and try to make some music with it. Will you hit it, blow into it, or pluck it? What kinds of materials could you use from your environment to make musical instruments? How are instruments played (plucked, hit, shaken, scraped)? How are they made? Put together a band of homemade instruments. Invite caregivers and other groups to attend a concert.

13. Types of Music

Content Connections:

History, economics

Guiding Questions:

- How have different ethnic groups influenced music styles?
- How is music used in everyday life?

Literature Connections:

East, Helen. *The Singing Sack: 28 Song-Stories from Around the World.* New York: HarperCollins. 2000.

Ehrhardt, Karen. *This Jazz Man.* Boston: HMH Books for Young Readers. 2015.

Taylor, Debbie A. *Sweet Music in Harlem*. New York: Lee & Low Books. 2013.

Encourage students to think about the different styles of music that they know (jazz, blues, hip-hop, rap, pop). Are there any rhythms that relate to each music style? Play a popular song on the radio and have students identify rhythms they hear, instruments, music style, and the message portrayed. Can a message be portrayed through different styles of music?

Examine various types of religious music. Compare the chants of monks to the chanting at mosques. Play music from a variety of church services. How is the music similar? How is it different? Are there any call-and-response songs? Are there any praise songs? How often is music used in each service? What is the purpose of the music?

Collect "food jingles" from advertisements on television. Why is music used on commercials? Have students write their own "jingles" for their favorite food. Encourage students to act out a commercial with music and without music. Which commercial makes you want to buy the product? Why?

For the younger students, play the song "Ah, vous dirai-je, Maman" by Mozart, which provides variations on the familiar tune for "Twinkle, Twinkle Little Star." Have students note that the song is played twelve different ways. Play several songs sung by Kidz Bop Kids (compilation albums featuring kids singing contemporary pop songs), then play the songs by the original artists and note the differences in musical styles.

The animated movie *Trolls World Tour* (directed by Walt Dohrn and David P. Smith, 2020, DreamWorks Animation) introduces six musical genres: funk, country, techno, classical, pop, and rock. The movie is filled with cultural metaphors and messages of positivity and inclusion. Play a variety of songs and ask students to classify the songs into one of the genres.

14. Storytelling with Music

Content Connections:

Geography, history

Guiding Questions:

- How can songs tell stories?
- Are there specific kinds of music that are associated with various cultural groups?

Literature Connections:

Gonzalez, Lusica. *The Storyteller's Candle/La Velita De Los Cuentos*. New
   York: Lee & Low Books, Inc. 2012.
Turk, Evan. *The Storyteller*. New York: Antheneum Books for Young Read-
   ers. 2016.

Music and storytelling go hand in hand in a variety of ways. Music can be
used to add emotion to a story.[4] For example, a minor key can suggest sad-
ness, or a major key indicate a happy mood. The change in tempo can relate
to suspense or tension. Different instruments can convey character. High
pitched notes can represent small or quick characters, while a low pitch might
indicate larger or slower characters. The classical composer Prokofiev wrote
a fairy tale symphony for children called *Peter and the Wolf* which uses musical instruments to represent characters: oboe for duck, clarinet for cat, French
horns for the wolf. Ask students, "Do songs tell stories?" To whom can the
message be directed? Do women and men tell the same kind of stories? What
kind of instrument might represent a chicken? A bear? A cow?

For younger students, teachers can take classic tales and use music to
enhance the stories. For example, with *The Three Billy Goats Gruff*, children
can use claves (tapping sticks) to make the sound of the billy goats "trip, trip,
trip" over the bridge. Other instruments can be used to make the sound of the
ugly troll under the bridge.[5] Write or find a musical story, such as the Kinder-
garten operetta for the story of *The Little Red Hen* (see appendix B), and have
students perform it at the end of the year for their caregivers. There are only a
few speaking roles in the operetta, so most of the class will sing the music. Ask
students to take their own favorite story and write it as a song or add musical
sounds to enhance the telling of the story. Adding costumes and movement will
enrich the storytelling experience and encourage sensory engagement.

15. Dance

Content Connections:

Geography, history

Guiding Questions:

- How can a story be told through dance?
- How have dances been used in various cultures?

Literature Connections:

Giles Andreae. *Giraffes Can't Dance*. New York: Cartwheel Books. 2012.
Flood, Nancy Bo. *I Will Dance*. New York: Antheneum Books for Young
   Readers. 2020.

Dances have been used for celebrations, religious rituals, storytelling, giving of thanks, preparation for war, and entertainment. Many agricultural people performed a rain dance during the spring planting season. Hula dancers tell stories of ancestral knowledge. The Maori danced the haka on battlefields to prepare warriors mentally and physically for the battle. Dance is a great way to foster interpersonal skills with students and introduce students to a particular culture.

In Louisiana, Cajun dancing is popular and there is typically a dance floor at most Cajun restaurants. The pioneers did square dancing at their socials. The Geisha dance is a symbol of femininity and nobility. Native American dances celebrated events, thanked the gods, or prepared warriors for battle. Share folk dances with students from various cultures and have students find similarities in the celebrations. Teach square dancing steps: do-sa-do, allemande, star, swing, bow, circle, forward, and back. Have students create a dance to represent an event in history, such as the Battle of Lexington and Concord.

Younger students can start with the "Limbo" dance from Trinidad. Hold a bamboo pole or broomstick and allow students to cross under the pole without touching it or the ground. Lower the pole for each pass. Liven up the dance by playing the "Limbo Rock" song recorded by Chubby Checker in 1962.

16. Whistle While You Work

Content Connections:

History, civics, economics

Guiding Questions:

- How is music used to inspire work?
- What kinds of events use music?

Literature Connections:

Locke, Betty. *Whistle While You Work: Land Without Music*. Scotts Valley,
   CA: CreateSpace Independent Publishing Platform. 2017.

Oelschlager, Vanita. *The Gandy Dancers: And Work Songs from the American Railroad.* Akron, OH: Vanita Books. 2015.

Many cultures use music to accompany their work. Occupations such as driving railroad spikes, mining, sailing, herding cattle, and picking cotton were made more efficient and coordinated through work songs. Often the work was tedious with poor working conditions. Songs allowed the workers to express their feelings about the job and to fight boredom. Often, the songs incorporated the movements and sounds of the job.

Country music is often considered the music of the working class. Students may be familiar with songs, such as "9 to 5" (Dolly Parton, 1980), "Coal Miner's Daughter" (Loretta Lynn, 1971), "Sixteen Tons" (Merle Travis, 1947), and "Hard Workin' Man" (Brooks and Dunn, 1993). Other work songs to share include "A Hard Day's Night" (Beatles, 1964), "A Spoonful of Sugar" (Robert Sherman and Richard Sherman, 1964), and "Whistle While You Work" (Frank Churchill and Larry Morey, 1937).

Ask students, "What work songs do you know? Why is music played in stores where people work? Are workers more productive when working to music? Do people buy more when they are in a store that plays music?" Introduce students to the Gandy dancers, railroad workers known for their synchronized movement when repairing track.

Tell students that athletes in Greece brought musicians to their practices. Ask students, "What benefit do you see in having music at a sport's practice? Is music played at sports events in your area? What kind of music is encouraged? How is music used at these events? Is the music broadcasted or provided by a group? How often is the music played?"

Have students to listen to music while they do chores. Ask students, "How does the music make you feel?" Encourage students to write "work" songs for regular chores that they do at home. Ask students, "What rhythms do you notice? How did the songs affect your work?"

For younger students, share songs from movies about work: "Whistle While You Work" and "Heigh-Ho" from *Snow White and the Seven Dwarves* (Walt Disney Productions, 1938); "A Spoonful of Sugar" from *Mary Poppins* (Walt Disney Productions, 1964); "Hakuna Matata" (no work) from *The Lion King* (Walt Disney Pictures, 1994). Play music when students do desk work and then have them vote on whether they feel more productive and enjoy their time more with music or without music.

NOTES

1. Jeffery A. Mangram and Rachel L. Weber, "Incorporating Music into the Social Studies Classroom: A Qualitative Study of Secondary Social Studies Teachers," *The Journal of Social Studies Research* 36, no. 1 (2012): 3–21.

2. "Too Late to Apologize—A Declaration" can be accessed at https://www .schooltube.com/media/Too-Late-to-Apologize-A-Declaration/1_vycawtpy.

3. "Bell," The Editors of Encyclopaedia Britannica, accessed August 2, 2020 at https://www.britannica.com/art/bell-musical-instrument.

4. Amanda Niland, "Musical Stories: Strategies for Integrating Literature and Music for Young Children," *Australian Journal of Early Childhood* 32, no. 4 (2007): 7–11.

5. Niland, "Musical Stories."

Chapter 3

Using Literature to Teach Social Studies

Dr. Paganelli

Reading is essential in social studies, which aligns with the mandate of many state standards that require the use of informational text. Teachers can help student comprehension of informational text by modeling the deconstruction of the texts to help students recognize major ideas, supporting details, important vocabulary, and the author's purpose.[1] However, it is important that the instruction addresses social studies content, not just reading skills. Students can be challenged to evaluate the credibility of the texts and note the sources use, as well as the author's purpose for writing the text. Teachers can make connections with students to primary and secondary sources and the ideas of interpretation.[2]

Learning through stories is a natural way to learn. Literature extends the social studies curriculum beyond textbook constraints. Stories allow readers to experience other times, other places, other people, and other cultures with empathy. Teachers can use exceptional literature to challenge stereotypes and encourage students to understand diversity. Students can find books that include diverse characters, yet explain social studies content. Biographies and memoirs can encourage discussions on family histories. Students can examine multiple perspectives, interpretations, and voices presented through literature to identify values, interests, and biases of authors.

An alternative to reading books is to introduce poetry in the social studies classroom. Poetry has a rich vocabulary and can be read in a short amount of time and in different ways. The rich emotion and syncopation of imaginative words encourage repetitive readings. Some models for poetry performance include the following:

- Read poems aloud to the class.
- Focus on words, meanings, and rhythms.
- Have students read aloud poems together in unison.
- Have students join in on repeated line or refrain.
- Divide students into groups for "call-and-response" type poems.
- Assign individual solo lines for readers.
- Put poems to music and sing them.
- Pantomime poems.[3]

Another common literature source is the newspaper. This multi-subject resource includes political cartoons, word puzzles, maps, and current events for use in a social studies classroom. Newspapers can be used to stimulate class discussions, introduce current trends and issues, promote critical thinking skills, and increase national and global awareness. The Internet also offers many newspaper-related resources. The Newspapers in Education website (https://nieonline.com/) provides online lesson plans and guides for using newspapers in many subject areas (30,000 lessons just for social studies!). The Paper Boy (https://www.thepaperboy.com/) provides over 10,000 online newspapers from around the world and can be used to read different perspectives on world events. Many communities also post their newspapers online.

Often, local businesses will pay for newspapers to be delivered weekly to classrooms.

Some ideas for newspaper use in the classroom include the following:

- Analyze editorials.
- Write a movie review.
- Use obituaries to write about achievements of the deceased.
- Discuss current events.
- Analyze political cartoons.
- Examine climate and weather.
- Read maps.
- Compare international issues.
- Teach vocabulary.
- Identify jobs and qualifications for positions.

Telephone books are another literature resource to utilize in the classroom, as they include several information items that connect to social studies: maps, time zones, community services, locations, and regional characteristics. In addition, students can compare telephone books over time, or compare telephone books from different communities.

Trade books are children's literature with curriculum content and can include folktales, historical fiction, myths, and biographies. Benefits of using trade books to teach social studies include the following:

- Richness of content and emotion
- Realistic stories set in the past
- Recreation of true incidents in the lives of real people
- Culture instruction, as well as, inherent values, beliefs, and customs

Folktales and origin stories are symbolic of the culture of peoples and also great tools to use in social studies. Folktales may consist of animal tales, magic tales, tall tales, or legendary tales. These tales represent the everyday life of people. In animal tales, specific traits may be assigned to certain animals, such as cleverness for a fox or malice for a spider. *Why Alligator Hates Dog* (Reneaux, 1995) tells the story of a dog who tricks alligator into coming on the porch for dinner, only to be chased away by Man. Magic tales involve quests for treasures or mighty deeds. *Aladdin and his Wonderful Lamp*

(Townley, 2015) from the Arabian Nights Adventure series tells the story of a poor boy who goes on an adventure to secure riches. Tall tales, often called "yarns," relate unbelievable events as if they were true, whereas, legendary tales relate to the exploits of heroes. Paul Bunyan, Pecos Bill, and John Henry arc familiar characters from these types of tales.

These types of literature connect to social studies and provide "hooks" to get students interested in learning the content. Most are easily obtained in the local library or through local resources. All children love a story, which makes using literature to teach social studies a win-win scenario.

ACTIVITIES USING LITERATURE
TO TEACH SOCIAL STUDIES

17. Geographic Book Reports

Content Connections:

Geography

Guiding Questions:

- How can books be represented through geography?
- What types of artifacts could represent a story?

Literature Connections:

Hinton, S. E. *The Outsiders*. New York: Speak. 2006.
McCloskey, Robert. *Make Way for Ducklings*. New York: Viking Kestrel Picture Books. 1941.

The *Guidelines for Geographic Education*,[4] published in 1984, introduced big ideas in geography known as the Five Fundamental Themes of Geography. These five areas of investigation are appropriate for teaching geography in the early grades. The themes consist of these ideas:

- *Location*: where a point is on earth's surface and why it is there
- *Place*: special features an area might have, such as climate, people, and landforms
- *Human/Environment Interaction*: how people react to and sometimes change their environment

- *Movement*: travel and communication with one another; movement of products and ideas
- *Regions*: areas of the earth that are alike in some way or another

Elementary teachers can use the mnemonic MR. HELP for the five themes of geography. A mnemonic device is a pattern of letters or numbers to aid in retention. Movement (M) would include ideas such as how do people, products, and ideas get from one place to another? Region (R) would ask, "What features set this place apart from other places?" Human/Environment Interaction (HE) notes how people's lives are shaped by places, or places are shaped by people. Location (L) would refer to where a place is, what it is near, and what direction to travel to reach the place. Place (P) would ask, "What physical and human features are present?"

Students can give a book report using the five themes of geography. The following is an example report based on the five themes:[5]

- Title and author of book: *The Outsiders*
- Where does the story take place (location)? Tulsa, Oklahoma
- What do things look like (place)? It is set in the 1960s in an urban area where the socioeconomic gap is evident in everything from housing and cars to clothes and hairstyles. The east side is representative of poverty and despair and the west side is representative of wealth and power.
- How have humans changed the environment or the environment changed humans? During several scenes they create havoc at parks or drive-ins where they throw things they do not pick up. They seem to just completely disregard their environmental impact, which was fairly typical of the 1960s.
- What is moving, why does it move, where is it going (movement)? Movement is super important in this story because movement determines success versus stagnation. Living on the east side signals poverty but if you can ever cross to the west side an increase in wealth would be a given. Neither side would ever admit to desiring a shift in movement if it meant living beside their rival gang, but I believe most people given the opportunity to shift socioeconomic ranks would jump at it. It is implied several times that movement is also possible via education.
- What are some characteristics that identify this place (region)? Gang violence seems to be common in the area as do petty crimes as well as more violent crimes. The split between rich and poor probably coincides with

the way the Arkansas River splits the city. Tulsa was actually the first inner city to develop an urban renewal program and it began about the time this book was released. New parks and family attractions were being created to attempt to diminish the gang violence and rejuvenate city facades.

For the younger students, a geographic activity with book reports is to give students a shoe box and ask them to place artifacts in the box and design a map to represent the story they read. Exchange shoe boxes and have students guess what they think the story is about. For example, for the book *Make Way for Ducklings* (McCloskey, 1941) students could place in the shoe box a rubber duck, a map of Boston, a policeman hat, and a picture of a pond.

18. Tradebook—Mama, Do You Love Me?

Content Connections:

Geography

Guiding Questions:

- How do Arctic animals adapt to their environment?
- What are the characteristics of an arctic environment?

Literature Connections:

Joosse, Barbara M. *Mama, Do You Love Me?* San Francisco, CA: Chronicle Books. 1998.
Le, Khoa. *The Lonely Polar Bear.* Mount Joy, PA: Happy Fox Books. 2018.
Napayok-Short, Suzie. *Kits, Cubs, and Calves: An Artic Summer.* Iqaluit, Nunavut: Inhabit Media. 2020.

Discuss with students the characteristics of food, clothing, travel, and shelter in an Arctic area. Inform students that you would like them to write down the names of all the Arctic animals they hear as you read aloud the trade book, *Mama, Do You Love Me?* (dog, ermine, lemming, musk ox, polar bear, ptarmigan, puffin, raven, salmon, walrus, whale, wolf). Ask students, what other arctic animals do you know (e.g., Arctic fox, penguin, reindeer, seal, snowy owl, moose)? Note that many of the animals have white fur/feathers to adapt to living in a habitat of ice and snow. Give each student a bar of white ivory soap and a plastic knife. Ivory soap is very soft and carves well. Tell students that you would like them to choose one Arctic animal to carve from the white soap. Spread newspaper on the tables to catch the shavings as students carve Arctic animals. After researching interesting facts about their animal, students must then present their soap animal to the class and share what they learned.

The younger students may have trouble carving soap, so an alternative might be to use white clay or playdough to form the Arctic animals. Sugar cubes could be used to make snow homes and white coconut or rice could be used to make snow habitats.

19. Newspaper—It's a Revolution!

Content Connections:

Geography, history, civics, economics

Guiding Questions:

- What information is available in a newspaper?
- How is the newspaper used today?

Literature Connections:

Hopkinson, Deborah. *Carter Reads the Newspaper*. Atlanta, GA: Peachtree Publishing Company. 2019.
Pilkey, Dave. *The Paperboy*. London: Orchard Books. 2016.

It is easy to get students interested in newspapers by publishing your own classroom newspaper. Introduce a topic, such as the Revolutionary War, then have students research and write articles as if they witnessed events from that time period. Include events such as the Boston Tea Party, Boston Massacre, Battle of Lexington and Concord, and the Stamp Act. Students will choose the headlines, which photographs to include, and even advertisements from the era. You can assign roles and responsibilities to students, such as the list below:

- Publisher—Teacher
- Editors—what stories go in, assign reporters, write opinions
- Reporters—cover stories

- Feature writers—special columns (e.g., advice column)
- Copy editors—look for mistakes
- Production department—determine layout of photos and articles
- Mechanical department—copy, staple
- Circulation department—distribute newspapers

Social studies is embedded throughout the printed news. For history, examine the centennial issue of a town newspaper or examine advertisements over time. For geography, examine the types of maps in newspapers or any environmental news. For civics, follow the campaigns of politicians or any government rulings. For economics, study the business section or the "for sale" ads.

Students can also do a newspaper scavenger hunt with printed or online newspapers. Place the students in teams and ask them to answer the following questions:

- Find an advertisement for a job. Write a description of what you would do to interview for this job.
- Find a home for sale. Why would you like to buy this home?
- Find a car you would like to buy. If you took five years (sixty months) to pay for the car, how much would you pay each month?
- Describe a local, national, and international event in the newspaper.
- What is on television at 7:00 p.m. (list every choice)?
- What is the weather going to be like tomorrow?
- What kinds of maps can you find?
- Summarize a letter to the editor. Who wrote it?
- Name something you could go to this week.
- Write the score for a sports game. Where did the game take place? [6]

The Library of Congress published a Teacher's Guide for analyzing newspapers.[7] One suggestion is to choose a news item, then find an article on the same topic published by a different source. Have students compare the coverage from the two sources and determine what is different, what is same, and what are possible explanations for the differences.

For the younger students, newspapers can be used for word searches, sequencing comic strip cells, or making paper maché models of the earth. Assign students to use the newspaper to find stories about people with different kinds of jobs. Ask students, what do people do in these kinds of jobs?

Have students cut out advertisements of things they would like to buy and add up the costs of the items. Discuss a class newspaper to be sent to parents. Ask students, what would parents like to know about our class?

20. Telephone Book Scavenger Hunt[8]

Content Connections:

Geography, history

Guiding Questions:

- What is the purpose of a telephone book?
- What replaces the telephone books today?
- How have telephone books changed over time?

Literature Connections:

Friddell, Claudia. *Grace Baker and Her Hello Girls Answer the Call: The Heroic Story of WWI Telephone Operators*. Honesdale, PA: Calkins Creek. 2021.
Grivis, Molly Levite. *Five Two, Five Blue*. Eakin Press. 1999.

Although telephone directors are difficult to find in this age of the Internet and cell phone directories, they are useful in teaching social studies. You can check out directories from libraries, or find them in businesses. Telephone directories provide a listing of subscribers in a geographic area. Typically, the information would include names, home, and business addresses, and sometimes the occupation of the person listed. Other information may include street directories, advertisements of businesses, lists of government officials, churches, schools, hotels, maps, time zones, and much more. Mail and phone directories can be accessed at the National Archives site (https://www.archives.gov/research/alic/reference/mail-and-telephone-directories.html).

Place students into groups and give each group several telephone books. Have students use the phone books to complete a scavenger hunt and answer questions, such as the following:

- In what part of the state is your city located?
- Where is the nearest city to your city?

- In what time zone is your city?
- What bodies of water are found near your city?
- What kinds of attractions are found in your area?
- What kind of recycling is found in your city?
- List some methods of transportation found in your city.
- What kinds of maps are in the telephone book?
- How many schools are in your area?
- What types of community help are available?[9]

You might discuss with students how operators were used to connect phones in the past. Have students research the "Hello Girls" from World War I. America's first female soldiers served on the front lines in the war as bilingual telephone operators.

For younger students, have them guess how many people they think are named "Smith" or "Jones" in their area. Project a phone book and count the names together. Talk about white pages (names of individuals and businesses) and yellow pages (classified advertising). Practice phone conversations with students. What do you say if the person calls a wrong number? What do you say if you need to leave a message for a return call?

21. Poetry

Content Connections:

Geography, civics

Guiding Questions:

- How can imagery be depicted with words?
- How do poems tell a story?

Literature Connections:

Prelutsky, Jack. *The New Kid on the Block*. New York: Greenwillow Books. 2013.

Silverstein, Shel. *Where the Sidewalk Ends: Poems and Drawings*. New York: HarperCollins. 2019.

The rhyme and rhythm of poems make this type of literature popular in any classroom. The use of poetry in social studies can open a world to students in which examining content or writing creatively makes learning powerful and vivid. Poems traverse topics from war to immigration to racism to natural wonders. Poetry allows for reading and recitation practice, discussions, analysis, summary writings, and more.

Poems can be used to describe confrontational challenges to popular beliefs, such as with Jack Prelutsky's "The New Kid on the Block." In this poem, a new kid in the neighborhood is a bully, with the surprise line at the end indicating that the bully is a girl.

Poetry can also be used to teach environmental concepts. Shel Silverstein's poem, "Sarah Cynthia Sylvia Stout Would Not Take the Garbage Out," encourages students to become aware of taking care of the environment. The words in this poem are very fun to say. The lines at the end indicate the fate of poor Sarah as the garbage she refused to take out piled on top of her.

The poem "The Man from Snowy River" is filled with descriptive geographic terms. Have students close their eyes and imagine the scenery as you read:

When they reached the mountain's summit, even Clancy took a pull,
It well might make the boldest hold their breath,
The wild hop scrub grew thickly, and the hidden ground was full
Of wombat holes, and any slip was death.
But the man from Snowy River let the pony have his head,
And he swung his stockwhip round and gave a cheer,
And he raced him down the mountain like a torrent down its bed,
While the others stood and watched in very fear.[10]

Discuss the images portrayed through the reading. You may even show a clip from the 1982 movie, *The Man from Snowy River* (directed by George Miller, 1982, 20th Century Fox), of this scene. Have students use rich vocabulary and write a poem about a significant event in history or a place they visited.

Of course, there are many poems that contain social studies content. Some interesting poems for study include the following:

- "Jackie Robinson"[11] by Lucille Clifton
- "When I am President"[12] by Felice Holman
- "Wars"[13] by Jean Little
- "Pledge"[14] by Carol Diggory Shields

- "Geography"[15] by Eve Merriam
- "Paul Revere's Ride"[16] by Henry Wadsworth Longfellow
- "Will V-Day Be Me-Day Too?"[17] by Langston Hughes

Have younger students write a two- or three-line poem to summarize something they learned in class. You might experiment with shape poems by writing a poem in the shape of the concept it represents. Encourage students to memorize poems and recite in front of their classmates. Talk about how poetry can comfort you, make you laugh, make you cry, and help you know and understand others.

22. Folktales

Content Connections:

Geography

Guiding Questions:

- How does a folktale represent a culture?
- How might the environment inspire a story?

Literature Connections:

Climo, Shirley. *The Irish Cinderlad.* New York: HarperCollins Publishers. 1996.

Ketteman, Helen. *Bubba the Cowboy Prince.* New York: Scholastic Press. 1997.

Martin, Rafe. *The Rough-Face Girl.* New York: Puffin Books. 1992.

Mayer, Marianna. *Baba Yaga and Vasilisa the Brave.* New York: William Morrow and Company, Inc. 1994.

Marceau-Chenkie, Brittany. *Naya, the Inuit Cinderella.* Yellowknife, Canada: Raven Rock Publishing. 1999.

San Souci, Robert D. *Little Gold Star.* New York. HarperCollins Publishers. 2000.

San Couci, Robert D. *Cendrillon.* New York: Simon & Schuster Books for Young Readers. 1998.

Schroeder, Alan. *Smoky Mountain Rose.* New York: Puffin Books. 1997.

Takayama, Sandi. *Sumorella: A Hawai'i Cinderella Story.* Honolulu, HI: The Bess Press. 1997.

Louie, Ai-Ling. *Yeh Shen: A Cinderella Story from China*. New York: Puffin Books. 1982.

Reneaux, J. J. *Why Alligator Hates Dog*. Little Rock, AR: August House LittleFolk. 1995.

Townley, Kelley. *Aladdin and his Wonderful Lamp*. United Kingdom: Harpendore. 2015.

Yue, Charlotte and David Yue. *Shoes: Their History in Words and Pictures*. Boston: Houghton Mifflin Harcourt. 1997.

The story of Cinderella is a tale that includes elements of magic, misfortune, love, and the universal struggle of good versus evil. The themes from the story appear in the folklore of many cultures. Begin the lesson by sharing with students that shoes are a part of clothing, which is a part of culture. Ask students to give their own definition of culture (the characteristics of a particular group of people, defined by everything from language, religion, cuisine, social habits, music, and arts). Ask students to state how many pairs of shoes they have in their closet. Note that culture is often described through various folktales from different places around the world. There are over 1,500 Cinderella stories. Ask students to guess which Cinderella tale is the oldest (*Yeh Shen* was written around AD 700 in China[18]).

Assign students to groups of four people. Give each student a different version of a Cinderella story to read: *Bubba the Cowboy Prince, Cendrillon, The Rough-Face Girl, Smoky Mountain Rose, The Irish Cinderlad, Little Gold Star, Baba Yaga and Vasilisa the Brave*. Assign group roles: reader—reads the story aloud to the group; recorder—answers questions; artist—draws symbol to represent story; map finder—places symbol on map for origin of story.

Questions to answer include the following:

- Who is the persecuted character in your story?
- What magic help is received?
- Who are the mean relatives?
- What type of shoe is involved, if any?
- What type of party or festival is involved?

Give students the comparison chart in appendix C. As you call on each group, say things like, "The reader in each group please tell me the name of your hero/heroine. The artist in each group tell me the magic help involved. The recorder in each group tell me what type of shoe is involved in the story." After comparing the Cinderella stories, ask the students the following questions:

- What symbol did your group use to represent your story? What might be another symbol?
- What cultural elements did you find in the story?
- What are some common characteristics of different cultures?
- What do names and clothing tell about a culture?
- What are some key patterns of Cinderella stories?

Have students write their own version of a Cinderella story, drawing from their personal backgrounds or an assigned culture. Show the students the book *Naya, the Inuit Cinderella* (Marceau-Chenkie, 1999) which was written by a fifth grader.

Most younger students have read the story of Cinderella or have seen one of the many movies about the character. Read three different Cinderella stories to students and then ask them to tell you what the stories have in common and how they are different. Take away one shoe from each student and have them come up with a story about how their shoe was lost. A good book to share with students is *Shoes: Their History in Words and Pictures* (Yue and Yue, 1997).

23. Origin Stories

Content Connections:

Geography, history

Guiding Questions:

- How is the environment connected to origin stories?
- Why are origin stories important to a culture?

Literature Connections:

Rohmer, Harriet and Mary Anchondo. *How We Came to the Fifth World: A Creation Story from Ancient Mexico.* San Francisco, CA: Children's Book Press. 1998.

Sandofa and Anderson, *The Origin of Life on Earth: An African Creation Myth*. Mt. Airy, MD: Sights Production. 1991.

Keens-Douglas, Richardo. *Mama God, Papa God: A Caribbean Tale*. Vancouver, Canada: Tradewind Books. 2016.

Strauss, Susan. *When Woman Became the Sea: A Costa Rican Creation Myth*. Hillsboro, OR: Beyond Words Publishing Company. 1998.

Wolkstein, Diane. *Sun Mother Wakes the World: An Australian Creation Story*. New York: HarperCollins. 2004.

Origin stories can offer a window into how people relate to their environment or their beliefs about the universe.[19] Share various origin stories with students: *How We Came to the Fifth World: A Creation Story from Ancient Mexico*; *Mama God, Papa God: A Caribbean Tale*; *Sun Mother Wakes the World: An Australian Creation Story*; *The Origin of Life on Earth: An African Creation Myth*; *When Woman Became the Sea: A Costa Rican Creation Myth*.

Ask students, why do you think the people of the Yucatan make sacrifices to the rain god? Why do you think island people tell stories that feature winds and storms? Why are light and dark representative of good and evil? There are a great variety of origin stories that provide explanations for earthly happenings. Challenge students to make connections between origin stories and geography, as well as investigate why specific places are mentioned in some stories. What aspects of a story relate to the geography of the land? What aspects of a story reflect the culture of the people telling the story? Why do you think this story was created?

For younger students, discuss that there are no rivers above ground in the Yucatan. The peninsula is made of porous limestone, through which rainwater drains underground. An activity to demonstrate the effect of rain on limestone is easily shown through placing drops of lemon juice on a piece of chalk and observing the erosion. Both rain and lemon juice are slightly acidic. Read an origin story from the Yucatan and explain how the lack of rivers influences the story. Discuss several Native American creation stories and ask students to find connections between the way of life of these peoples and the environment on the stories.

24. Literature Circles

Content Connections:

History

Guiding Questions:

• What guides the perspective of a story?
• Why should you read more than one perspective?

Literature Connections:

Bader, Bonnie. *Who Was Christopher Columbus?* London: Penguin Workshop 2013.
Krensky, Stephen. *Christopher Columbus (Step into Reading 3).* San Diego, CA: Harcourt School Publishers. 1991.
Sis, Peter. *Follow the Dream: The Story of Christopher Columbus.* New York: Knopf Books for Young Readers. 1991.
Yolen, Jane. *Encounter.* New York: Voyager Books. 1992.

Literature circles are a powerful teaching tool using books.[20] Assign students into groups and assign each group one book to read. Everyone in the group needs to contribute to the discussion of the book. Teachers can choose the topic and provide books with varying perspectives. For example, students can be assigned books to read on Columbus: *Encounter; Who Was Christopher Columbus?; Christopher Columbus;* and *Follow the Dream: The Story of Christopher Columbus.* Have each group come up with questions to share, discuss illustrations, and share readings of passages to demonstrate the perspectives portrayed in the books. Ask students, "How is Columbus portrayed in the books? How are Native Americans portrayed? Does the book have a bias toward Columbus or the Native Americans?"

Young students can choose books to discuss in a literature circle. Assign roles to group members (read passage, lead discussion, write questions, illustrate, report out) and assign questions for students to answer. Design a rubric to evaluate student participation, comprehension of the book, and cooperation among group members. Have students create bookmarks that summarize information they learned from the discussions.

NOTES

1. Judy Britt and Mandi Howe, "Developing a Vision for the Common Core Classroom: What Does Elementary Social Studies Look Like?," *The Social Studies* 105, no. 3 (2014): 158–163, DOI: 10.1080/00377996.2013.866930.

2. Ava L. McCall, "Teaching Powerful Social Studies Ideas Through Literature Circles," *The Social Studies* 101, no. 4 (2010): 152–159, DOI: 10.1080/00377990903284104.

3. Sylvia M. Vardell, "Poetry for Social Studies: Poems, Standards, and Strategies," *Social Education* 67, no. 4 (2003): 206–211.

4. Joint Committee on Geographic Education, *Guidelines for Geographic Education: Elementary and Secondary Schools*, Washington, DC: National Council for Geographic Education and Association of American Geographers, 1984.

5. Book report by Melissa Cockriel in assignment for course, Geographic Skills and Concepts for Teachers, Western Kentucky University, Fall 2019.

6. Activity shared by Teacher Consultants with the Louisiana Geography Education Alliance (LaGEA).

7. "Teachers Guide: Analyzing Newspapers," Library of Congress, accessed July 15, 2020, https://www.loc.gov/static/programs/teachers/getting-started-with-primary-sources/documents/Analyzing_Newspapers.pdf.

8. Adapted from lesson "Reach Out and Touch Someone with Geography," by teacher Deborah Tatum.

9. Activity shared by Teacher Consultants with the Louisiana Geography Education Alliance (LaGEA).

10. Excerpt from Andrew Barton, Paterson, *The Man From Snowy River and Other Verses*. University of Sydney Library (1997). Accessed January 29, 2020 from http://adc.library.usyd.edu.au/data-2/v00001.pdf.

11. Poem from R. R. Knudson, *American Sports Poems*. New York: Orchard, 1996.

12. Poem from Felice Holman, *The Song in My Head*. New York: Atheneum, 1985.

13. Poem from Jean Little, *Hey World, Here I Am!* New York: HarperCollins, 1986.

14. Poem from Carol Diggory Shields, *Lunch Money and Other Poems About School*. New York: Dutton, 1995.

15. Poem from Eve Merriam, *The Singing Green*. New York: Morrow, 1992.

16. Poem can be accessed at the Poetry Foundation, https://www.poetryfoundation.org/poems/44637/the-landlords-tale-paul-reveres-ride.

17. Poem can be accessed at poets.org, https://poets.org/poem/will-v-day-be-me-day-too.

18. Information from The World of Chinese accessed from https://www.theworldofchinese.com/2015/03/ancient-chinese-cinderella-story/ (March 22, 2015).

19. S. Kay Gandy and Kathleen Matthew, "Origin Stories: Geography, Culture, and Belief," *Social Studies and the Young Learner* 22, no. 4 (2010): 25–28.

20. McCall, "Teaching Powerful Social Studies."

Chapter 4

Using Visual Media to Teach Social Studies

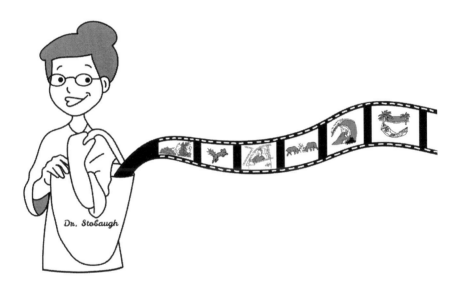

Visual media can help students get the point easier than with words. Rather than teach or read about a rose, bring a rose into the classroom and allow students to see it, smell it, touch the petals and thorns. A visual image of the rose is the second-best way to teach about the flower. Students learn in different ways, but younger children are very much visual learners. Observing a familiar place through pictures initiates memories and taps into prior knowledge. Visual media of photographs, cartoons, and film are primary sources readily available to classroom teachers.

Photographs are a primary source that can be used in detective work. Studying images gives students the opportunities to use observation, inference, and communication skills. Photographs occur in a particular place at a certain point in time, taken by a particular photographer for a specific purpose.[1] Students can become "time" detectives in social studies with the use of visual media. Photographs of everyday history are readily available at the National Archives (https://www.archives.gov/) and the Library of Congress (http://www.loc.gov/pictures/) websites. The early "Brownie" camera developed by the Eastman Kodak Company was sold at a price of one dollar, as it was intended to be used by children.[2] Later, instamatic cameras contributed to the ease of creating photographs. The built-in flash, fixed aperture, and easy to load film allowed the average person to document everyday life. Today, students can use phones or tablets as cameras. Have students use their observation and communication skills with photographs by answering questions, such as the ones below:

- What is shown in the image?
- What type of paper is the image printed on?
- Is the photography in color or black and white?
- What time period in history does the photograph represent? How do you know?
- Why was this photo taken?
- What can we learn from this photo?[3]

Students can use photographs to compare the past and present or put eras in sequence.[4] With their investigations skills, students can compare their findings as individuals or from group work, make inferences, reach broad conclusions, and develop questions for further research. Historical photographs can provide a means for learning content and create student interest in the past. For example, students could examine photographs to discern similarities and differences in segregated schools.[5] Students could answer questions such as "What do you notice about the classroom, the teacher or the students? How would you feel if you were a student in these classrooms? Which classroom would you want to be in and why?"

Cartoons are another visual tool that can be used in the social studies classroom. Children are visual by nature, and with cartoons, language is not a barrier. Cartoons present the big idea and provide a platform for the use of analytical and critical thinking skills. This tool can be used to motivate struggling readers and inject humor into the lesson. Cartoon elements include symbolism, irony, humor, and exaggeration. Teachers can use cartoons in assessment, in discussions, or as a hook to introduce a lesson.[6]

Students could be asked to evaluate cartoons with questions, such as the following:

- What objects and people do you see in the cartoon?
- Where is the place shown in the cartoon?
- When do the events in the cartoon occur?
- What is happening in the cartoon?
- What adjectives describe the emotions or feelings portrayed in the cartoon?
- What is the message of the cartoon?
- How would you change the cartoon to communicate the message more clearly?[7]

Political cartoons often appear on state or national assessments. Teachers can use these types of cartoons in the classroom to introduce point of view, caricatures, symbolism, social injustices, or economic abuses. Students could be asked to construct a cartoon depicting an opposing view to the one presented.[8] Some guidelines for choosing cartoons include avoid risqué or offensive cartoons, choose cartoons that have a basis in truth and a moral purpose, and choose cartoons that connect to content and are not drawn solely for comic relief.[9]

Film has been used both to entertain and to provide documentary information. Classic films can be used as a window to the past. Often, popular books that students read are made into movies. Because filmmakers take liberties with facts or print, students can research the accuracy of movies or compare the film to the book to see what has been changed. The Internet Movie Database is an excellent source to find out information on casts, crews, plot summaries, trivia, reviews, and movie trailers.

Choosing the right movie or documentary is important in the classroom. Administrative approval is needed to prevent any legal ramifications, as teachers need to assure the appropriateness of the film and the objectives for its use. English as a Second Language (ESL) students or students with special needs may need films with subtitles. Some films may cause unwanted visual or auditory stimulation. Below are some guidelines for showing appropriate or relevant movies:

- Watch the movie before you show it to students. Make notes of significant scenes. You may not want to show the whole movie.
- Give students a purpose for watching the movie. Be sure to research the historical accuracy of the movie.
- Watch the movie with your students. Point out significant events and answer questions.
- Allow parents to make the choice whether their child can watch the movie or not. For students who cannot watch, allow them to go to another room and research the movie and its historical context so they may participate in the discussion.
- Check with your school and district administration regarding film policies.
- Develop questions to be answered after the movie and include a participation grade.[10]

Producers and distributors typically submit their films to a Rating Board established by the Motion Picture Producers and Distributors of America. The Board examines sex, violence, nudity, adult topics, language, and drug use before assigning the G, PG, PG-13, R, or NC-17 ratings. This helps parents decide what films are appropriate for their children and will help the teacher decide what is appropriate for the classroom.

Streaming services, such as Netflix, Hulu, Disney+, and Amazon Prime, provide limitless access to TV series and movies. This allows teachers the ability to show examples of clothing and living conditions of royalty and commoners, address the battle by Senator Joseph McCarthy to find and eliminate Communists in the United States, or have students analyze how the X-Men movie series relates to the persecution of a people.[11]

Films and TV series serve as virtual windows into the past.[12] In the early 1900s, films were used not only for entertainment but also for information and news. Through newsreels and instructional films, students can evaluate fashion styles, economy, and culture from the past: secretaries using typewriters and desk phones, housewives cooking without microwaves. The Newsreel Archive can be found at https://www.youtube.com/user/newsreelarchive/videos.

ACTIVITIES FOR USING VISUAL MEDIA
TO TEACH SOCIAL STUDIES

25. Small-Town Images

Content Connections:

Geography, civics, economics

Guiding Questions:

- How do people affect the environment and the environment affect the people of a town?
- How do images indicate the characteristics of a town?

Literature Connections:

Davies, Monica. *Photographs throughout American History (Journey to the Past: Investigating Primary Sources)*. Milwaukee: Gareth Stevens Publishing. 2019.

Griesmer, Russell. *My Hometown*. Bloomington, MN: Picture Window Books. 2015.

Give each group of students a packet of photographs or folder of digital images from a small town and ask them to make inferences about physical and human characteristics about the place to answer the following questions:

- What jobs do people do in this town?
- What do people do for recreation in this town?
- Would you classify this town as urban, suburban, or rural?
- Would someone viewing these pictures see the same things you do? Why or why not?
- How can photographs show the history of a town?
- How did humans alter this place?[13]

Students will explain how they used the photographs to obtain information and make inferences and generalizations about the place.

Require students to go out to a town they visit with their families and photograph specific physical or human characteristics that might represent that town. When students share their work in the classroom, ask questions such as "Does the size of the town matter for jobs that are offered? Does the town have a main square? Is this town known for anything in particular?"

For the younger students, collect photographs of various types of homes and how they are constructed: single structures, apartments, condos, mobile homes, brick, log, wood, siding. Connect types of homes to environmental factors (e.g., urban areas have less space for single structure homes). You might also share photographs of various types of transportation in a city: taxi, subway, bus, car, bicycle, train, motor scooters. Discuss with students what is free to ride or which modes you must pay to travel on.

26. Cartoons and Comic Strips

Content Connections:

History, civics

Guiding Questions:

- How might cartoons portray political issues?
- How important is text versus images?

Literature Connections:

Ball, Jzikah. *Cartoon President: Team Patriot.* Independently Published. 2018.

Smiley, Jess Smart. *Let's Make Comics! An Activity Book to Create, Write, and Draw Your Own Cartoons.* New York: Watson-Guptill. 2018.

Students can use critical thinking skills to read and create political cartoons. Introduce students to symbolism that is often used with cartoons: dove (peace), stereotypes (dishonest lawyers), irony, caricatures (exaggerated ears), analogies (comparison to Cold War), juxtaposition (politician next to a dollar sign).[14] Remind students that political cartoons represent key events and attitudes of a certain time period. Political cartoons use emotional appeals and other techniques to persuade the reader to accept the opinion of the creator.

One activity with political cartoons could be to white out commentaries or remove captions from the cartoons and ask students to come up with their own ideas as to what the cartoon should say.[15] How does the message change for each of the student-created captions? How persuasive are the student commentaries? What groups might the cartoon have appealed to? Show students examples of editorial cartoons (seeks to persuade the opinion of the media to its readers). How do they differ from political cartoons?

Cartoons can be used to document a visual history, teach sequencing skills, tell a story, indicate opinions, and introduce students to humor and culture. Do we all laugh at the same things? Remove the last frame on a cartoon and ask students to draw the ending. Does the ending change the message? Challenge students to create cartoons of an historical event and leave off the last frame. Exchange with a partner and finish each other's cartoon.

For the younger students, introduce students to a variety of cartoon comic strips at the website https://www.gocomics.com/. Provide each student with blank paper and have them draw several story boxes. Have students think about something funny that happened to them and try to draw two or three pictures to represent the events. Encourage students to create dialogue for any characters that they draw. Exchange papers and share out with the class. Sequencing skills can be taught by cutting up frames of simple comic strips and asking students to put them in the correct order.

27. Comic Books

Content Connections:

History, civics

Guiding Questions:

- Why are comic books a good way to explore societal issues?
- What comic book characters have been made into movies? Why are these types of movies so popular?

Literature Connections:

Cameron, Neill. *How to Make Awesome Comics*. Oxford, United Kingdom: David Fickling Books. 2017.
Solomons, David. *My Brother Is a Superhero*. London: Puffin Books. 2017.

Comic books utilize cartoons to create longer stories, often with messages for societal issues. For example, the X-Men comics document the experiences of a marginalized people (mutants) in an oppressive society. Some comics have dealt with issues such as drug abuse and suicide with strong lessons for the young reader. Batman and Spiderman faced the loss of a loved one; Magneto (from X-Men) was a member of a concentration camp; Captain America fought against the tyranny of the Nazis. Events in the characters' lives greatly impacted the choices they made and the heroes they became.

Illustrations in comic books give context to the story line. Ask students, would the story remain the same without the illustrations? If not, how would it change? Discuss why comics are an effective way to discuss societal issues. Have students draw their own comics to include a message of importance.

Discuss with students some popular comic series that have been made into movies: Batman, X-Men, Ant-Man, Aquaman, Avengers, Black Panther, Captain America, Captain Marvel, Daredevil, Dr. Strange, Fantastic Four, Guardians of the Galaxy, Iron Man, Men in Black, Spiderman, Superman. Ask students to infer the messages from these comic movies and discuss the popularity of the movies.

For younger students, comic books are available in simplistic forms. The My First Comic Book series includes books on feelings, such as *I'm Sunny* and *I'm Grumpy* by Jennifer and Matthew Holm (2016). Another book written in comic style is *Jellaby: The Lost Monster* (Soo, 2014) which addresses issues of bullying, absent parents, and grief and loss. The fifty issues of *Tiny Titans* (Baultazar and Aureliani) comic books focus on the school-aged DC Comics characters. The comics can be used to start discussions of issues that children might face.

28. Let's Go to the Movies

Content Connections:

History, civics

Guiding Questions:

• How have movies influenced culture throughout history?
• What is the difference between a documentary and a movie?

Literature Connections:

Frost, Shelley. *Kids Guide to Movie Making: How Kids Can Produce & Direct Movies that Audiences Will Love*. London: DK Children. 2020.

Stoller, Brian Michael. *Smartphone Moviemaker*. Somerville, MA: Candlewick. 2017.

Start a movie club after school or assign movies to watch outside of class. Students can then watch the movie, summarize it, and make connections to what is being learned in class. Have students discuss what is accurate or inaccurate about the character portrayals or scenes. How are Native Americans portrayed in films? How has the role of women changed in films?

In class, show clips of movies to interest students in eras of history. Set up the background for the showing and give students several questions to answer after watching the scene. Teachers may assign readings to go along with the clip and introduce new vocabulary. Listed below are examples of several movies and miniseries with historical settings:

- *John Adams* (directed by Tom Hooper, 2008, HBO Films)—TV miniseries based on life of John Adams
- *Bury My Heart at Wounded Knee* (directed by Yves Simoneau, 2007, HBO Films)—Movie on the displacement of Native Americans in nineteenth century.
- *Band of Brothers* (directed by Phil Alden Robinson, Richard Loncraine, Mikael Salomon, David Nutter, Tom Hanks, David Leland, David Frankel, and Tony To, 2001, HBO Films)—TV miniseries depicting the Army Airborne Easy Company, 506th Regiment of the 101st Airborne Division during World War II.
- *Thirteen Days* (directed by Roger Donaldson, 2000, Beacon Pictures)—Movie based on Cuban Missile Crisis and the Kennedy administration.
- *Apollo 13* (directed by Ron Howard, 1995, Director, Universal Pictures)—Movie based on the true story of the Apollo 13 mission and NASA's "successful failure" in quest for the moon.
- *All the President's Men* (directed by Alan K. Pakula, 1976, Wildwood Enterprises)—Movie about the two *Washington Post* reporters who uncover the Watergate scandal which leads to the resignation of President Nixon.
- *Selma* (directed by Ava DuVernay, 2014, Plan B Entertainment, Harpo Productions, Pathé, Cloud Eight Films, Ingenious Media)—Movie that depicts the march from Selma to Montgomery, Alabama, in 1965 as part of a campaign to secure equal voting rights.

Students can create their own documentaries or movies through moviemaker apps or even photo apps with video. Explain that a documentary is a movie that is nonfiction and captures reality. Some examples for students to film might be nature documentaries, historical reenactments, reporter interviews, music videos, or adventure stories. Introduce students to movie making basics:

- *Have a concept*—What will your movie be about? Is it a comedy or drama? Will it need character actors? Props? Costumes? Is it based on facts or completely fiction? Where will the movie take place?
- *Write a script*—There should be a beginning, middle, and end to your story. Using a storyboard will help you lay out the sequence. Remember to keep the plot simple.
- *Shoot the movie*—Follow the storyboard and get all the shots you need. Be sure to get lots of footage!
- *Edit the movie*—What needs to be cut out or reshot? Should you add music or sound effects? Titles or closings? Are the lighting and audio effective?[16]

If you do not want to take the time to have students shoot an entire movie, ask students to design a movie trailer that would highlight in one minute what a movie might be about.

Most younger students are familiar with YouTube videos and would be delighted to participate in a simple video project. Make a series of videos to introduce new students to your classroom. Your students could model lining up at the door to go to lunch, putting away materials, turning in homework, and so on.

29. Civic Photography

Content Connections:

Civics

Guiding Questions:

- How can a photograph represent citizenship?
- How are photographs helpful as a primary source?

Literature Connections:

Jacquart, Anne-Laure. *Photo Adventures for Kids: Solving the Mysteries of Taking Great Photos*. San Rafael, CA: Rocky Nook. 2016.

O'Neill, Alexis. *Jacob Riis's Camera: Bringing Light to Tenement Children.* Honesdale, PA: Calkins Creek. 2020.

Rockliff, Mara. *Lights! Camera! Alice! The Thrilling True Adventures of the First Woman Filmmaker.* San Francisco, CA: Chronicle Books. 2018.

To bring democracy into a photography assignment, have students take cameras around their school, home, or community and take pictures of their ideas of democratic citizenship (e.g., social and moral responsibility, political literacy, community involvement, working for the common good, shared decision-making, equal opportunity).[17] Students must then explain how their photos represent democratic citizenship. For example, a photo of the classroom rules might represent to students the idea of shared decision-making if they had a part in choosing the rules. A rotating student job chart might represent the idea equal opportunity. Ask students to describe citizenship that might be photographed at a mall, in a business, or even on a playground.

For younger students, show a variety of pictures of community helpers: police officer, firefighter, mail deliverer, doctor, nurse, teacher, paramedic, baker, bus driver, and so on. Take photographs of tools that community helpers use and have the students match the tool to the helper. Have a dress-up day and make an art exhibit of photographs of students dressed as community helpers.

30. Movie Issues

Content Connections:

Geography, history, civics, economics

Guiding Questions:

- Why are movies a good way to explore societal issues?
- What issues today should be made into movies? Why?

Literature Connections:

Nagara, Innosanto. *A Is for Activist.* New York: Triangle Square. 2013.

Paul, Caroline. *You Are Mighty: A Guide to Changing the World.* New York: Bloomsbury Children's Books. 2018.

Movies can be used to address political, social, and economic issues with topics such as the following:

- Race—*The Long Walk Home* (directed by Richard Pearce, 1990, Dave Bell Associates, New Vision Films)
- Changing roles of women and men—*Kramer vs. Kramer* (directed by Robert Benton, 1979, Columbia Pictures)
- Nuclear weapons—*Thirteen Days* (directed by Roger Donaldson, 2000, Beacon Pictures)
- The environment—*WALL-E* (directed by Andrew Stanton, 2006, Pixar Animation Studios)

Students can be assigned into groups to prepare presentations that include a summary of the movie (with emphasis on historical context), an analysis of the movie's view of the period, and a brief excerpt to illustrate the analysis. Discuss with students how accurately the film represents the episode it portrays, missing perspectives, and how the movie may differ if it were made today.[18] Ask students to consider issues important to them that should be made into movies.

There are a variety of great movies to use with younger children to introduce issues for discussion:

- *Inside Out* (directed by Pete Docter and Ronnie del Carmen, 2015, Pixar Animation Studios)—teaches about emotions and how to navigate a new home and school
- *The Lorax* (directed by Chris Renaud and Kyle Balda, 2012, Illumination Entertainment)—teaches about the plight of the environment and the Lorax who speaks for the trees
- *Finding Nemo* (directed by Andrew Stanton and Lee Unkrich, 2003, Pixar Animation Studios)—teaches the importance of listening to parents and courage in the face of adversity
- *The BFG* (directed by Steven Spielberg, 2016, Sony Pictures Studio)—teaches not to be prejudiced toward people based on how they look
- *FernGully: The Last Rainforest* (directed by Bill Kroyer, 1992, FAI Films and Kroyer Films)—teaches about logging and pollution

Discuss the perspectives from the movie and have students draw what they learned. Display drawings and have students do a gallery walk and place stickers on the drawing they relate to the most.

NOTES

1. Ellen Sieber, "Teaching with Objects and Photographs: Supporting and Enhancing Your Curriculum, A Guide for Teachers," Mathers Museum of World Cultures (2012): 15–23, accessed May 14, 2020, https://mathersmuseum.indiana.edu /doc/Tops.pdf.

2. Sieber, "Teaching with Objects and Photographs."

3. Sieber, "Teaching with Objects and Photographs."

4. Keith C. Barton, "A Picture's Worth: Analyzing Historical Photographs in the Elementary Grades," *Social Education* 65, no. 5 (2001): 278–283.

5. Theresa M. McCormick and Janie Hubbard, "Every Picture Tells a Story: A Study of Teaching Methods Using Historical Photographs with Elementary Students," *Journal of Social Studies Research* 35, no. 1 (2011): 80–94.

6. Richard Ostrom, "Active Learning Strategies for Using Cartoons and Internet Research Assignments in Social Studies Courses," *Social Studies Review* 43, no. 2 (2004): 61–64.

7. Nancy P. Gallavan, Angela Webster-Smith and Sheila S. Dean, "Connecting Content, Context, and Communication in a Sixth-Grade Social Studies Class through Political Cartoons," *The Social Studies* 103 no. 5 (2012): 188–91, DOI: 10.1080/00377996.2011.605644.

8. Joseph Eulie, "Creating Interest and Developing Understanding in the Social Studies through Cartoons," *Peabody Journal of Education* 46, no. 5 (1969): 288–290.

9. C. Frederick Risinger and Ray Heitzmann, "Using the Internet to Teach about Political Cartoons and Their Influence on U.S. Elections," *Social Education* 72, no. 6 (2008): 288–290.

10. John Burkowski Jr. and Xose Manuel Alvarino, "Teaching Social Studies Through Film," The Education Fund, accessed April 23, 2020 file:///C:/Users/ stp16282/Downloads/Teaching%20Social%20Studies%20Through%20Film%20 (2009).pdf.

11. William B. Russell III, "The Art of Teaching Social Studies with Film," *Clearing House* 85, no. 4 (2012): 157, DOI: 10.1080/00098655.2012.674984.

12. Karl A. Matz, and Lori L. Pingatore, "Reel to Real: Teaching the Twentieth Century with Classic Hollywood Films," *Social Education* 69, no. 4 (2005): 189.

13. Adapted from lesson by Bryan Runyan, teacher consultant with the Louisiana Geography Education Alliance and Pat Robeson, teacher consultant with the Maryland Geographic Alliance.

Chapter 4

14. Heather LeBlanc, "Political Cartoons: 7 Ways to Step Away From the Lecture Podium & Revitalize Your Social Studies Classroom," accessed June 10, 2020, https://www.brainyapples.com/2018/06/12/political-cartoons-in-the-social-studies -classroom/.

15. Risinger and Heitzmann, "Using the Internet to Teach about Political Cartoons."

16. "Seat Up: Kids Guide to Making Movies," accessed July 23, 2020, https:// seatup.com/blog/kids-guide-to-making-movies/.

17. Cynthia Szymanski Sunal, Lynn Allison Kelley, Andrea K. Minear, Dennis W. Sunal, "Elementary Students Represent Classroom Democratic Citizenship Experiences via Photos," *The Journal of Social Studies Research* 35, no. 2 (2011): 191–216.

18. Andrea Libresco, "Past and Present Imperfect: Recent History and Politics Go to the Movies," *Social Education* 81, no. 3 (2017): 148–153.

Chapter 5

Using the Environment to Teach Social Studies

Dr. Huss

Students deserve authentic, relevant, and meaningful learning opportunities. Using the environment as a starting point to teach social studies concepts connects students to the responsibilities of stewardship and civic life. Students can become active citizens and help solve community problems. As the teacher emphasizes hands-on, real-world learning experiences, students develop stronger ties to their communities and gain an appreciation for the natural world. Students will employ critical thinking skills—questioning, investigating, forming hypotheses, interpreting, analyzing, developing conclusions—as they work to solve problems in their own living environment.

Introduce students to the idea of place-based learning through questions such as the following:

- How does our community take care of those unable to care for themselves?
- What developed and potential energy resources are in our area?
- Where does our garbage go?
- How does water get to the tap in our homes?
- How might a hurricane affect local roads and public services?
- What types of disaster should we prepare for in our community?

Social studies content is readily available in the local environment. Historical information can be obtained by examining the cultural heritage of the area, using place as three-dimensional primary documents, and acquainting students with historical resources available. Civics can be understood through the places where governance is conducted, social justice movements, and issues in the community. Geography can be studied through patterns of movement, physical, and human characteristics, and determining why places in the area matter. Economics is prevalent in changing technology, work life, commerce, and the market industry.

Projects for community action can come from a variety of topics: homelessness, hate crimes, poverty, disabilities, immigration, human rights, bicycle safety, water quality, landfills. Teachers will want to share with students some community action projects that others have done:

- Mosquito control without pesticides
- Illustrated walking tour booklet of a historic neighborhood
- Data collection on ground-level ozone damage to plants in an area
- Production of magazine about local Appalachian culture
- School gardens to provide lunchroom vegetables
- Energy audit of schools and creation of new school policies that reduced energy usage and costs

- Curbside recycling service
- More trash cans in a park to reduce littering
- Community education campaign to reduce pollution

It takes time and commitment to come up with a viable plan to take action to improve and sustain the local environment. The best way to go about it is to set up tasks for various students or groups of students. The Earth Force Community Action and Problem-Solving Process[1] is a good model to follow. The first step is to examine the local community (school or town) and determine any issues that might be a problem. Look for cause and effects of the problem. What would the students like to see changed? Once students articulate what they want to change, then they can begin strategic planning to implement the change. The teacher can set up interviews with individuals who know about the selected issue. Students can seek out resources (newspaper archives, websites, historical archives) to understand the history of the issue. The action plan can include direct service (serving food at a homeless shelter, reading to senior citizens, creating a walking trail) or indirect service (bake sale, food drive, letter-writing campaign). In order to guide the decision-making process, teachers can create a chart of questions to answer:

- How much class time or out of school time can be required?
- What funds are needed or budgeted?
- Which ideas are most interesting to students?
- What tasks can each student handle?
- Which activities will have the most impact on the community?
- Which ideas will students be able to carry out?
- How can the project be sustained?
- How can the results be evaluated?

After the plan has been implemented, a time of reflection and evaluation is necessary to give thought to the impact of the activity. Ask students, "What did we learn? What impact did we make? Now what?" Plan to celebrate the success of the project and recognize students for their hard work. Include a public presentation to increase awareness of the community/environmental issue.

ACTIVITIES USING THE ENVIRONMENT
TO TEACH SOCIAL STUDIES

31. The American Trail System[2]

Content Connections:

Geography, history

Guiding Questions:

- What are some issues that land management agencies might face?
- What Federal agencies are involved in land management?

Literature Connections:

Dek, Maria. *A Walk in the Forest*. New York: Princeton Architectural Press. 2017.

Farrell, Alison. *The Hike*. San Francisco, CA: Chronicle Books. 2019.

Oswald, Peter. *Hike*. Somerville, MA: Candlewick. 2020.

Thermes, Jennifer. *Grandma Gatewood Hikes the Appalachian Trail*. New York: Harry N. Abrams. 2018.

In the 1920s, citizens on both coasts of the United States began putting together the groundwork for the National Trail Systems. The National Trail System Act of 1968 designated the Appalachian and the Pacific Crest as the first two National Scenic Trails. Later, the National Historic Trails and the National Recreation Trails were designated.

Divide students into groups and have each group research a trail system. Trails to research may include The Arizona Trail, The Appalachian Trail, The Continental Divide Tail, The Great Western Trail, The North Country National Scenic Trail, The Pacific Crest Trail, The East Coast Greenway, The Paiute ATV Trail, The Pacific Northwest Trail, The American Discovery Trail. Students will be required to answer questions about the trail and produce a map of the trail (either digital or drawn). Each group will design a display board featuring facts about the trail and the map of the trail. Have each group create a commercial advertising their trail. Groups may use display boards in the commercial.

Questions each group must answer include the following:

- What is the name of the trail?
- Which states does the trail cross?

- Does the trail journey north/south or east/west?
- Does the trail cross any private land?
- Is the trail complete? If not, how much of the trail is complete? What is the projected completion date?
- Who envisioned the trail?
- What types of recreation are allowed on the trail (e.g., hiking, mountain biking, ATV riding, horseback riding)?
- Is there a map available for the trail online?
- What organizations manage the trail?

Lead a class discussion in the uses of public lands. Discuss controversies of land use with such issues as motorized versus nonmotorized forms of recreation. Which trails researched allow only hiking? Why would some areas only allow hiking? Have students research trails available in their own state. Plan a class hike on a nearby trail, and/or contact local organizations to adopt a trail.

For younger students, you might plan a short hike. Instruct students on safety and conservation rules. Be sure to take along water and sunscreen. Plan frequent stops to talk about what the students can see, smell, or hear. Tell students to respect creatures and plants and do not disturb the environment. Students may want to bring a sketchbook or camera to document their surroundings. Pocket-sized field guides to birds, trees, or flowers are readily available at any bookstore. Be sure to get copies of the trail map and teach students how to read the map. Following the hike, have students draw or write about the things they saw or experienced.

32. Environmental Exercise: Reduce Your Waste

Content Connections:

Geography, civics, economics

Guiding Questions:

- How can we reduce the amount of trash we produce?
- Where does our garbage go?

Literature Connections:

French, Jess. *What a Waste! Trash, Recycling and Protecting Our Planet.* London: DK Children. 2019.

Gibbons, Gail. *Recycle! A Handbook for Kids*. New York: Little, Brown Books for Young Readers. 1996.

Javernick, Ellen. *What if Everybody Did That?* Seattle: Two Lions (Amazon Publishing). 2010.

Showers, Paul. *Where Does the Garbage Go?* New York: HarperCollins. 1993.

Silverstein, Shel. *Where the Sidewalk Ends*. New York: HarperCollins. 1974.

Van Allsburg, Chris. *Just a Dream*. Boston: Houghton Mufflin. 1990.

Zimmerman, Andrea and David Clemesha. *Trashy Town*. New York: Harper Collins. 1999.

Because children are the leaders of tomorrow, educating them today to become responsible users and protectors of the environment will result in a more positive future for our planet. This activity will motivate students to explore ways humans can produce less waste and encourage them to learn more about recycling.

Read the poem "Sarah Cynthia Sylvia Stout Would Not Take the Garbage Out" (Silverstein, pp. 70–71). Brainstorm with students the problems with having too much garbage (air, land, and water pollution; no place to put the waste; shortage of natural resources). Demonstrate the concept of reduction with a balloon (air is reduced when you let it out).

Ask students to begin saving everything they would normally throw away in the next twenty-four hours. Give each student a grocery bag and ask them to put trash from home, school, and any other activities into the bag for one entire day. Share with students that the average American throws away four pounds of garbage every day. Weigh each student's bag of trash and record the results with a graph. Brainstorm ways to reduce the amount of trash (reduce, recycle, reuse). Place plastic on the floor and spread out the trash. Challenge students to see how much of the trash they could eliminate by using the three Rs.[3]

Talk about things we can do to help save the earth:

• Recycle
• Find places to take your old things (consignment stores)
• Use cloth instead of paper towels; handkerchiefs instead of tissue
• Do not leave water running when you brush your teeth
• Plant a garden

- Throw garbage in the trash, not on the ground
- Bring a bag when you go shopping
- Use rechargeable batteries
- Turn out lights when you are not using them

Read the book *Where Does the Garbage Go?* (Showers, 1993). Find out where wastes are disposed of in your state. Discuss recycling and composting with students. Introduce landfills and find out if your community has a landfill. Ask students, "Does our town recycle? What is recycled? Do we have any landfills in our area?"

Many younger students may be familiar with Oscar the Grouch from the television show *Sesame Street* who lives in a garbage can. Collect various types of clean trash and tell the students that Oscar needs to sort his trash by plastics, paper, and metal. Dump the trash in the middle of the floor and let students sort by category. Introduce students to the concept of recycling (old products are used to make new products) and brainstorm ideas for using the trash to make something useful (e.g., decorate a can to make a pencil holder). Make a game by labeling trash cans and having students throw items in the correct can.

33. Postcards from the Edge: Endangered Species[4]

Content Connections:

Geography, history, civics

Guiding Questions:

- How can we help save endangered species?
- Why is it important to help with species and habitats?

Literature Connections:

Clinton, Chelsea. *Don't Let Them Disappear.* New York: Philomel Books. 2019.

Jenkins, Martin. *Under Threat: An Album of Endangered Animals.* Somerville, MA: Candlewick. 2019.

The U.S. Fish and Wildlife Service is a bureau within the Department of the Interior whose mission is to work with others to conserve, protect, and enhance fish, wildlife, and plants and their habitats. The bureau manages the

93-million-acre National Wildlife Refuge System with more than 530 individual refuges, wetlands, and special management areas. Among its key functions is the protection of endangered species. Since the arrival of Europeans in North America, hundreds of species have become extinct. The population of many more declined due to loss of habitat, degradation of the environment, pollution, pesticide use, and other factors. Within the United States, over 700 species of animals and almost 2,000 species of plants are listed as threatened or endangered.[5] The United States took a giant step toward saving plants and animals with the passage of the Endangered Species Act in 1973.

Have students analyze reasons why they should help with species and habitats. Assign each student the task of creating a postcard of an endangered species in their state. You can use 5 × 7 index cards to represent the postcards. Species listed as threatened or endangered by state are available at https://www.fws.gov/endangered/index.html. By clicking on the scientific name of the species, students can view a species profile. Information includes status details, life history, recovery plans, Federal Register documents (e.g., final rules listing the species, critical habitat designation, and designation of experimental populations), habitat conservation plans, petitions received, and current news releases. Have the students include facts on the postcard about the endangered species and a drawn or cutout picture of the endangered species.

Postcards can be displayed on a bulletin board or used to create a game. Discuss reasons for protecting endangered species (helps protect a healthy environment, helps protect sustainable economies and a good quality of life, and protecting our Nation's heritage is a fundamental American value). Discuss ways students can help:

- Learn about the endangered species in your area
- Volunteer at a national wildlife refuge or park
- Make your home wildlife friendly (secure garbage cans, feed pets indoors)
- Remove non-native plants from your yard
- Avoid using chemical pollutants (herbicides and pesticides)
- Buy sustainable products
- Start a petition to save a species
- Write a letter to a government official to take action to protect a species
- Create an animal calendar with information on endangered species
- Hold fundraising events and donate to help save a species[6]

For young students, show the documentary "Island of Lemurs: Madagascar" (directed by David Douglas, 2014, Warner Bros. Pictures), which focuses on the endangered lemur species. An educator guide accompanies the documentary and can be found at http://islandoflemurs.imax.com/downloads/educator_guide_complete.pdf. There is also an animated movie called "Madagascar" (directed by Eric Darnell and Tom McGrath, 2005, DreamWorks Animation) that follows a group of New York zoo animals who end up in Madagascar and must adapt to living in the wild. Have students draw a map of Madagascar and detail habitats that would encourage the comeback of lemurs.

34. Superheroes of Public Land Management[7]

Content Connections:

Geography, civics

Guiding Questions:

- Who are the "superheroes" of land management?
- What are some challenges that land management agencies face?

Literature Connections:

Rohmer, Harriet. *Heroes of the Environment: True Stories of People Who Are Helping to Protect Our Planet.* San Francisco, CA: Chronicle Books. 2009.
Tariq, Ambreen. *Fatima's Great Outdoors.* London: Kokila. 2021.

Public lands are one of America's greatest treasures. One-third of the country belongs to its citizens. Over 600 million acres include national parks, national wildlife refuges, national forests, national seashores, monuments, marine sanctuaries, trails, underground mineral reserves, and national grasslands. All fifty states have at least one area designated as public lands. These lands not only proved places for outdoor recreation and education but also protect ecosystems and provide natural resources.[8]

Children today are losing their connection to the land, and thereby their concern about its welfare. America led the way to set aside land for the public: in 1864, Yosemite became the first state park; in 1872, Yellowstone became the world's first national park; in 1906, Devil's Tower in Wyoming became the first national monument; and in 1924, the Gila Wilderness Area of New Mexico became the first wilderness set aside.

With the Federal Land Policy and Management Act (FLPMA) of 1976, Congress established a policy to retain public lands in public ownership, to identify and inventory their resources, and to provide for multiple and sustainable uses. The purpose of this activity is to introduce students to public land management agencies and their missions. Students will research a management agency and design a superhero to represent the agency.

Have students research the various uses of public lands (mining, farming, forestry, camping). Ask students questions such as, "What makes a hero? Who are your heroes?" Public lands belong to all American people, but they are also home to thousands of species of fish and wildlife, and a diversity of plant species. Historic and archaeological sites, as well as scenic wonders, are a part of the many natural and cultural resources that can be found on public lands. Several departments of the U.S. government manage public lands for us. These lands represent a priceless legacy that must be conserved for future generations. We truly need superheroes to preserve America's backyard.

Assign students the task of researching a land management agency and designing a superhero to represent that agency. Students would need to include the symbol for the agency somewhere on the costume of the superhero and incorporate facts about the agency into the design. Some descriptions of land management agencies are included below:

- *Bureau of Land Management* (BLM)—agency within the U.S. Department of the Interior that manages outdoor recreation, livestock grazing, mineral development, and energy production on public lands
- *USDA Forest Service*—agency with the Department of the Interior that manages public lands in national forests and grasslands
- *National Park Service*—preserves natural and cultural resources and values of the national park system for the enjoyment, education, and inspiration of this and future generations
- *U.S. Geological Survey*—largest water, earth, and biological science and civilian mapping agency
- *Bureau of Reclamation*—manages, develops, and protects water and related resources in an environmentally and economically sound manner in the interest of the American public.

Have students share their superheroes with the class. The designs could be posted on a bulletin board. Ask students to share ideas of skills and training needed to be a land manager. Discuss with students some of the challenges that land management agencies face (endangered species, growing population, environmental conditions, fires). Students can debate issues concerning the use of off-highway vehicles, such as motorcycles, trail bikes, snowmobiles, or all-terrain vehicles, on public lands. Other issues to debate include digging pipelines through public lands or securing public lands to build the wall between Mexico and the United States.

Curriculum-based programs using national parks with links to lesson ideas and parks in your area are available at www.nps.gov/learn/curriculum.htm. Other public lands organizations that provide educational resources include the U.S. Department of Agriculture Forest Service (www.fs.fed.us/kids/), the BLM (www.blm.gov/education/), and the U.S. Fish and Wildlife Service (https://www.fws.gov/refuges/education/teachersResources.html).

In 1994, Public Lands Day (PLD) was established to build partnerships for the stewardship of public lands. Held annually on the fourth Saturday in September, PLD gives thousands of volunteers the opportunity to restore and improve public lands around the country. This event is hosted by the National Environmental Education Foundation and can inspire environmental stewardship with students and teachers.

For younger children, visit webcams posted by the National Park Service at https://www.nps.gov/subjects/watchingwildlife/webcams.htm. Students can watch Old Faithful, a geyser at Yellowstone National Park, which is known for its regularity of eruption, or view wildlife up close through the hundreds of webcam views. Discuss with students how park rangers and volunteers help maintain national and state parks for the public to enjoy. Show the arrowhead symbol of the Park Service. Tell students that the Park Service wants a new symbol. Discuss the ideas presented by students and allow them to draw their designs.

35. Backyard Habitats[9]

Content Connections:

Geography, civics

Guiding Questions:

- How can we create a habitat at home or in a schoolyard?
- How have landscapes disturbed the balance of ecosystems?

Literature Connections:

Barrett-O'Leary, Marilyn. *Oh No! Hannah's Swamp Is Changing*. Baton Rouge, LA: Louisiana Sea Grant College Program. 2002.

Cherry, Lynne. *The Great Kapok Tree: A Tale of the Amazon Rain Forest*, Boston: HMH Books for Young Readers. 2000.

Il Sung Na. *Welcome Home Bear*. New York: Knopf Books for Young Readers. 2016.

Kurlansky, Mark. *World Without Fish*. New York: Workman Publishing Company. 2014.

This activity introduces students to the concept that a habitat can be in their own backyards or schoolyards. In 1973, the Backyard Wildlife Habitat program was established in an effort to create an awareness of how land management can have major effects on wildlife. This program offered a certificate from the National Wildlife Federation for anyone who created a habitat in a backyard, on a balcony, at a workplace, or in a schoolyard.

Introduce to students the concept that a habitat is the place in which an animal or plant species lives. Explain how habitat loss is the number one threat to wildlife. The conversion of natural areas into landscapes has disturbed the balance of ecosystems and has resulted in drastic reduction of habitat and the disappearance of many species of wildlife. Discuss human/environment interaction and how land management has affected wildlife.

Assess the space you are considering to be a habitat. List native and non-native plants. Which plants might provide food or nesting places? It is important to restore native plant communities to the area. Native plants require less fertilizer, water, pest control, and maintenance than non-native plants. Contact the state or local plant society to find native species to your area. A website that is helpful in identifying plants is the Invasive Plant Atlas of the United States found at https://www.invasiveplantatlas.org/.

Examine water in the planned area to be a habitat to make sure it is available and unpolluted. Wildlife may need water for drinking, bathing, breeding, or cover. Consider adding evergreen trees or shrubs to provide year-round protective cover. Logs and rocks also offer good cover or places to raise young. Use mulch to conserve soil moisture. Control pests by organic means. For instance, birds, bats, and ladybugs eat insects.

Everyone who provides the basic habitat elements (food, water, cover, and places to raise young) and who takes steps to conserve natural resources in their yard may apply for a Certified Wildlife Habit. Fill out an application for certification, attach photos or a sketch of your habitat area, and send to the National Wildlife Federation. Apply for certification at https://www.nwf.org /garden-for-wildlife/certify. If you plan the habitat in your schoolyard, apply for certification at https://www.nwf.org/schoolyard/.

Introduce students to the OSAE strategy:[10] observe, speculate, analyze, and evaluate. Visit a habitat and develop a series of questions for each OSAE category. *Observation* questions might include the following: "What do you really see? What is the land use? What color is . . .? What is . . . near? What is . . . made of?" For *Speculation* questions ask the following: "Why is it there? What does it represent? What is its role? What forces do you think caused . . .? How do you think . . .? Why do you think . . .?" *Analysis* questions will use comparison: "How does this compare to . . .? What sources could explain . . .? What evidence can be gathered to determine the role of . . .?" For *Evaluation* questions ask the following: "Is this a wise use of land? How might it be better used? How well is . . . working? Does it accomplish the purpose of . . .?" Students are then taken to the site, divided into small groups, and given the questions to answer and a clipboard for easy writing, or you might create a virtual field trip with questions and photographs. Afterward, a debriefing session encourages further analysis and evaluation about the experiences encountered.

For younger students, introduce biomes: rainforest, wetlands, desert, marine, tundra. Describe the types of animals and plants that would live in each biome. Divide the students into five groups and let each group color one biome on a large poster sheet. Use magazines to cut out pictures or allow students to draw or create various plants and animals. Make a game in which students choose a plant or animal and match to the biome. Ask students, "What might happen if part of the rainforest burns? If the desert suddenly got too much rain?" Move an animal or plant to a different biome and ask students if the animal might survive.

36. Legacy of the American West[11]

Content Connections:

Geography, history, economics

Guiding Questions:

- How have stories of Native American, African American, and Hispanic cowboys been written out of history?
- What geographic factors influenced the movement of cattle and settlement of ranches?

Literacy Connections:

Brett, Jan. *Armadillo Rodeo*. London: Puffin Books. 2004.

Charles, Tami. *Fearless Mary: Mary Fields, American Stagecoach Driver*. Park Ridge, IL: Albert Whitman & Company. 2019.

Iverson, Peter. *When Indians Became Cowboys: Native Peoples and Cattle Ranching in the American West*. Norman, OK: University of Oklahoma Press. 1997.

Lester, Julius. *Black Cowboy, Wild Horses: A True Story*. New York: Dial Books. 1998.

Pinkney, Andrea Davis. *Bill Pickett, Rodeo-Ridin' Cowboy*. Indianapolis, IN: HMH Books for Young Readers. 1999.

Our understanding of cowboys has for the most part been informed by movies, television shows, dime-store novels, and Wild West shows. The stereotypical images of the "white" cowboy and the red-skinned "savages" do not pay homage to the cowboy culture and history which are a product of men and women of many ethnicities. Cowboys are found in many countries around the world: "huasos" in Chile, "gauchos" in Argentina, "jackaroos" in Australia, and "llaneros" in Venezuela. Their "horse" may be a pickup truck or helicopter, but cowboys still ride the range.

With social studies, teachers can integrate the study of cowboys and their environment in a variety of ways:

- Ask students to dress as cowboys or to bring in artifacts of cowboy life (bandana, saddle, spurs, chaps, hat, boots, lariat).
- Cook up a Chuck Wagon feed of Old West cuisine, such as baked beans, biscuits, and beef jerky. Discuss why these particular foods were prevalent with cowboys.
- Read cowboy poetry or sing cowboy songs: "The Streets of Laredo," "Home on the Range," "Red River Valley," "Tumbling Tumbleweeds."

Have students create their own writings. Cowboys sang songs to soothe the restless cattle. What in the environment would cause cattle to be restless? Play Aaron Copeland's musical compositions called "Rodeo" and "Hoe-down." Ask students to describe the images that the music invokes.

- Research the many jobs of cowboys (wrangler, trail cook, bronco buster, foreman, roper, top hand) and reflect on the discrimination against various groups. Discuss how the environment impacted each job.
- Practice tying knots for lassos. View videos on lasso throwing. Research the famous lariat thrower, Will P. Rogers.
- Map some of the famous trails, such as the Old Chisholm Trail, Santa Fe Trail, and Old Spanish Trail. What dangers did the cowboys face on the trails? What environmental factors influenced trails?
- Study land use, cattle drives, and markets to focus on the economics of ranching. What was the best way to move cattle? Why?
- Research cattle brands and how they could be altered by rustlers. Have students create their own cattle brands.

Introduce students to the idea that there were many Native American, Hispanic, and African American cowboys in the Wild West. Early Spanish missionaries trained Native Americans as cattle herders. The Civil War generated many African American cowboys, as white ranchers went off to fight in the war. When the Spanish introduced horses and cattle to the Americas, large haciendas were established in Mexico. American cowboys learned how to break a bronc, ride a herd, and throw a lariat from the Mexican vaquero. The National Park Service has a series of lessons available on The American Cowboy at https://www.nps.gov/tapr/learn/education/upload/cowboy %20trunk.pdf.

No lesson on cowboys would be complete without teaching about the rodeo. This sporting competition evolved out of working practices of the cowboy to see who was the best in roping herding and riding. Cowboys and cowgirls compete in tie-down roping, steer wrestling, saddle bronc riding, bull riding and barrel racing. Host your own rodeo competition. Students could try to lasso chairs or barrel race with wheel barrels. Talk about famous rodeo riders, such as Bill Pickett who created the "bulldogging" method of wrestling steers. The Bill Pickett Invitational Rodeo Association has published a Rodeo Activity Booklet at http://ncacowboy.com/BPIR_Rodeo_Activity_Booklet.pdf.

For younger students, stick horse racing can be part of your rodeo. Students can create fringed vests from paper bags, tie knots with yarn, and make trail mix for the long roundup. Show students various paintings and photographs of cowboys from the Library of Congress website at https://www.loc.gov/search/?in=&q=cowboy+pictures&new=true&st=. Have students describe the environment in the artifacts. Note the wide-open plains, grass, and water sources needed for cattle. Have students create a cowboy mural across a wall in your classroom.

37. War and Peace

Content Connections:

Geography, history, civics, economics

Guiding Questions:

- How do people's lives change with war?
- How is the environment affected with war?

Literature Connections:

Breckler, Rosemary. *Sweet Dried Apples.* Boston: Houghton Mifflin Company. 1996.
Cha, Dia. *Dia's Story Cloth.* New York: Lee & Low Books, Inc. 1998.
Heide, Florence Perry and Gilliland, Judith Heide. *Sami and the Time of the Troubles.* New York: Clarion Books. 1995.
Polacco, Patricia. *Pink and Say.* New York: Scholastic, Inc. 1994.

War metaphors are interspersed in our language: "He shot down my idea"; "She attacked my plan." A lack of education on war produces disinterested citizens who are not concerned with military engagements. Warfare is an event that people should work hard to prevent from happening in the future. It is important that students understand the causes and realities of war on the environment and the consequences for the lives of citizens in war-torn nations.

Divide the students into groups. Assign each group a "war" book to read: *Pink and Say*—Civil War; *Sweet Dried Apples*—War in Vietnam; *Dia's Story Cloth*—War in Laos; *Sami and the Time of Troubles*—War in Lebanon. Group roles could be reader (read the story aloud to the group), scribe (ask questions and record answers), artist (illustrate what group thinks about war and its impact on people), reporter (share summary of story), and displayer (to describe the artwork).

Questions to be answered could include the following:

- What do you think the lives of the characters were like before the war?
- How has war affected the environment?
- What feelings do the characters have about the war?
- How can the environment cause war?
- When and where did this story take place?

Ask students would they be willing to go to war to defend themselves or their family. Have students think about how people justify war. Discuss with students current wars happening in the world and the effects on the country in which the war is happening and the effect on U.S. citizens. Note that the United States has been involved actively in war since September 11, 2001. Talk about marches, speeches, boycotts, and other forms of activism to prevent war. Invite a veteran to speak to students.

Introduce younger students to Alfred Nobel who left his fortune to establish the Nobel Peace Prize to give to any person who works to encourage peace in the world. Discuss how a committee chooses a winner each year, and how a person must be nominated for the award. Tell students that no one can nominate herself/himself. Ask students to talk about conflicts that might happen at home or school and what they could do to encourage peace. During the week, have students watch for others who are peacekeepers and nominate them for the class Nobel Peace Prize.

NOTES

1. Earth Force information accessed September 12, 2020 at https://earthforce.org/caps/.

2. Adapted from lesson "American Trail System" by S. Kay Gandy accessed at http://americanfrontiers.net/lessons/.

3. Adapted from lesson "Just a Dream: How People Change the Environment," in Laurel R. Singleton, *G is for Geography: Children's Literature and the Five Themes* (Boulder, CO: Social Science Education Consortium, 1993): 75–78.

4. Adapted from lesson "Postcards from the Edge" by S. Kay Gandy accessed at http://americanfrontiers.net/lessons/.

5. Environmental Conservation Online System, U.S. Department of Fish and Wildlife Service, accessed August 4, 2020 at https://ecos.fws.gov/ecp/listedSpecies/speciesListingsByTaxGroupTotalsPage.

6. Adapted from "10 Easy Things You Can Do to Save Endangered Species," Endangered Species Coalition, accessed August 4, 2020, https://www.endangered.org /10 easy things you can do to save endangered species/, and "Raise Awareness," National Geographic Kids, accessed August 4, 2020, https.//kids.nationalgeographic .com/explore/nature/mission-animal-rescue/raise-awareness/.

7. Adapted from Lesson "Public Lands Superheroes" by S. Kay Gandy accessed at http://americanfrontiers.net/lessons/.

8. S. Kay Gandy, "Public Lands in the Elementary Curriculum," in *Stewardship of Public Lands: A Handbook for Educators* (New York: American Association of Colleges and Universities, 2010): 151–157.

9. Adapted from lesson "Backyard Habitats" by S. Kay Gandy accessed at http://americanfrontiers.net/lessons/.

10. Walter Kimball, ed., "So, You Want to Read a Landscape . . ." by C. L. Salter, Chapter 6 in: *Spaces and Places: A Geography Manual for Teachers* (Washington, DC: Geographic Education National Implementation Project, 1995): 73–78.

11. Adapted from article, S. Kay Gandy, "Legacy of the American West: Indian Cowboys, Black Cowboys, and Vaqueros," *Social Education* 72, no. 4 (2008): 189–193.

Chapter 6

Using the Community to Teach Social Studies

Community involvement determines the strength of a person's commitment and attachment to their own community. This attachment influences the sense of stewardship to a place. Citizens would be less likely to deface or pollute the environment of a place they cared about. Often, the history of local businesses can intrigue students and develop a sense of pride in the community. In one community, Delta Airlines started out as a crop-dusting service and later carried passengers, Coke was first to be placed in a bottle, and the first million-dollar hotel in the state was built. Teaching with places that students encounter daily will add to their appreciation of their surroundings and serve to connect students to their communities.

Getting students involved in local issues offers them the opportunity to learn social studies through political action. Democratic participation offers students authentic examples of the institutions that influence their lives.[1] In the local community, students can explore how funds are raised and spent, the types of legal issues faced, the structure and roles of various government members, and services provided for community members.

There are many different research projects that students can think about: bridges; neighborhoods; town founders; natural disasters; regional architecture; local artists, writers, or musicians. Students can answer questions such as the following:

- What did kids do for fun in the past?
- How has our town been affected by war? By natural disasters? By disease?
- Who lived here before the town was established?
- What history does my family have in this town?

Cemeteries are an exceptional community teaching tool. They are accessible and interdisciplinary. Almost every community has a nearby cemetery that is an educational resource as well as a historic site. The age of a community, its ethnic composition, and the impact made by immigration can be determined by "reading" gravestones. The style of headstones, the symbolism of their art, and their inscriptions reflect religious beliefs, social class, and values, as well as cultural change over time. Cemeteries document the history of war, disease, ethnicity, and burial customs. Students need to be taught that any cemetery or burying ground is an important part of individual and collective history and needs to be treated with reverence, respect, and care.

Communities are open textbooks to learn social studies. Main streets offer a window into architect, commercial and civic enterprises, land use, and change over time. Monuments and memorials indicate important people and events. Festivals celebrate the image of the community. All content areas of social studies can be readily found in the local community.

ACTIVITIES FOR TEACHING SOCIAL STUDIES USING THE COMMUNITY

38. Main Streets[2]

Content Connections:

Geography, history, civics, economics

Guiding Questions:

- How can "main street" be used to explain the history of a community?
- What primary sources can be found in our community?
- What are the functions of buildings on main street? How have the architectural styles changed over time?

Literature Connections:

Abrahamson, Terry. *The Blues Parade*. Abrahamson Press. 2020.

Goodall, John S. *The Story of a Main Street*. New York: Margaret K. McElderry. 1987.

Kelly, Linda Lowe. *Mice on Main*. Tucker, GA: United Writers Press, Inc. 2008.

Main streets are often synonymous with small-town America, a place of security, and pride. The history, politics, economics, and geography of a community can be explored on a tour of any main street. Architecture, monuments, place names, newspapers, and maps can serve as primary sources for students to comprehend the change over time that takes place on a main street. The size and location of a building can explain its role in a community. Architectural details, materials, even the placement of doors and windows can explain a building's role by implying messages like "authority," "prosperity," or "welcome." Certain kinds of buildings have become metaphors for the beliefs, values, and aspirations of society.

Students can participate in a plethora of activities on a local main street:

- Determine use of buildings in the past/present by using some of the following: Sanborn maps, aerial photographs, historical photographs, interviews with tenants
- Identify land use

- Collect oral histories from local residents
- Study the influence of railroads, rivers, and highways on the location of main streets
- Note focal points and spatial layouts
- Research toponyms (street and building names) and iconography (monuments and memorials)
- Examine Sanborn maps (fire insurance) to research building use over time
- Document architectural styles
- Identify commercial and civic functions of buildings
- Interview business owners on main street
- Analyze the relation of the courthouse to the Central Business District (CBD) (center, adjacent, removed)
- Measure the length and width of main street (using a measuring wheel)
- Create a model of main street

Show students pictures and discuss characteristics of various styles of architecture: Federal, Greek, Italianate, Art Deco. Introduce architectural terms: buttress, colonnade, cupola, facade, gable, parapet, portico. Have students research various architects: Frank Lloyd Wright, Louis Sullivan, Alexander Thomson, Andrew Palladio, and Buckminster Fuller. Students then complete the template in appendix D to document the architecture of their own local "main street."

Take students to visit the courthouse, public library, bank buildings, and newspaper offices to find primary documents related to growth on main streets. Assign students to groups. One group will measure the length and width of the town main street. Another group will use the Sanborn maps and/or aerial photographs to document the changes in building use, structures, and the main street over time. A third group can complete the templates in appendix E for structures on the courthouse square and appendix F for building use on the main street. Have groups meet back in the classroom to compare information gathered and compile the results into a report.

Ask students to create posters of their town main street from the past and present and make predictions for the future. Based on aerial photographs, have students draw a map of the main street from a "bird's-eye" view. Students can visually record each vista and each structure on the main street through digital or some type of photography. Students will note dates on buildings and identify architectural styles of buildings. Ask students to categorize all the buildings according to function (commercial, civic, residential). Then sort the buildings by common visual characteristics. Have students investigate the styles and prepare a report on their findings. Students will answer questions such as the following:

- What is the location of main street (latitude and longitude)? Why is it located there?
- What is main street near?
- What are the townspeople's relationships to main street?
- How has immigration had an impact on this area?
- What are some of the characteristics of the region around main street (e.g., area, language, political divisions, religions, and vegetation)?
- How have people changed the environment to better suit their needs?
- What factors determine building use or location?
- How has life changed on main street over the years?[3]

In the classroom, have students collect photographs or other digital images, map land use, conduct research on building materials and street names, and identify festivals that take place on or near the town main street.[4] Students can develop a multimedia presentation depicting the history of the main street in their community and include a guided walking tour of noted buildings and landmarks. The tour should include a map, important building names and usage, significant landmarks, quotes from local residents, important historical events and people, and photographs from the community.

Inquire of students what they think might be future changes to the community. Students will serve as researchers, recorders, interviewers, and photographers and document the change over time of their community. The final product will be presented to caregivers and local community members. Have students create a time capsule of items that would be representative of their town. Hold a ceremony and bury the time capsule. Document information in the library as to when the capsule should be opened and where it is located.

Encourage students to put together several geocaches (containers with a small prize inside) and hide them on noted areas of their main street, or have earthcaches (learn about a place on the earth) for participants to find noted areas/buildings/monuments on the street. Mark the exact latitude and longitude of the caches using a GPS unit and post these markings on https://www

.geocaching.com/play, or on the school website. Students should plan to host a day for participants to go find the caches.

Assign students a building on main street to adopt and study. Ask students to report on the building by identifying its function and style and use over time. Include a photo and interviews with inhabitants or workers. Students may ask the business owners questions such as the following:

- What has your building been used for over the years?
- How long has your family owned this building?
- What is the architectural style?
- How does parking affect your business?
- Why did you choose to open a business here, rather than at a place like a mall?

The interviews will provide students with a context for understanding continuity and change on main street through the eyes of those who live and work there.

Next, students will make a brochure to put in the building to introduce its history to visitors. Have students dress appropriately for various time periods in the history of the city and present "talks" on life on their main street for that particular era. A good website to visit is the main street National Trust for Historic Preservation (www.mainstreet.org).

For younger students, show a picture of main street at Disney World. Talk about the various buildings located on the street and the parade that happens daily. Share pictures of a small-town main street and an urban main street. Have students look for similarities and differences. If possible, take students to your own town main street area. Ask students, do we have any parades downtown? Why do people go downtown? Collect milk cartons and cardboard boxes for students to build a replica of downtown.

39. Cemeteries

Content Connections:

Geography, history

Guiding Questions:

- How can cemeteries be used to explain the history of a community?
- What are some ways that people honor the dead?

Literature Connections:

Eliot, Hannah. *Día de los Muertos*. New York: Little Simon. 2018.
Gaiman, Neil. *The Graveyard Book*. New York: HarperCollins. 2010.
High, Linda Oatman. *The Cemetery Keepers of Gettysburg*. London: Walker Children's Books. 2007.
Twain, Mark. *The Adventures of Tom Sawyer*. Garden City, NY: Dover Publications. 1998.

Cemeteries can also be used as a tool to teach social studies. Life spans, religions, generations, ethnicity, war, and disease are evident in the community through the examination of tombstones.[5] Over time, people have created many ways to bury and honor the dead. The way communities deal with their deceased depends on their technology, climate, topography, and cultural beliefs. Some students may be afraid to visit a cemetery, as movies often portray cemeteries as spooky or eerie places. However, cemeteries are a unique part of communities and can provide a plethora of ideas for the classroom teacher. To stimulate student interest, the teacher could read selected passages from literature that take place in graveyards, such as in Mark Twain's *The Adventures of Tom Sawyer*.

There are many different activities that students could do at cemeteries such as the following:

- Write about the history of the community based on facts collected from the cemetery
- Document a recurrence of names on tombstones that are reflected in local buildings or parks
- Photograph unusual tombstones
- Create maps of the various areas of the cemetery
- Study burial customs and funeral traditions from various cultures, such as Day of the Dead
- Calculate the ages at which people died and/or graph death rates by decade
- Draw a sketch, and measure and record the height of gravestones
- Find markers for soldiers of wars and/or research other types of marker symbols
- Volunteer for grave marking projects or other events that cemetery trustees have in place (e.g., placing flags on veteran graves on Memorial Day)

When visiting cemeteries, have students record name, gender, birth and death dates, and materials used to make tombstones. Students could answer questions such as the following:

- What is the earliest date you found on a tombstone?
- What symbols do you see on tombstones? What do you think the symbols mean?
- What is the longest life span you found? The shortest life span?
- What mementos have people left to honor the dead?

Planning a field trip to a cemetery includes explaining proper protocol to students: stepping around graves, treating gravestones with care, being respectful of mourners, leaving no trash. Students need to wear proper clothing for outdoor work. Check with the caretaker to make sure there are no graveside services going on during the time of your visit. Inquire about rules at the cemetery and gather historical information and maps of the cemetery before visiting. Check to see if the cemetery allows gravestone rubbings and any other protocols they have in place.

Explain to students the various types of cemeteries that exist: military, church, public, family, ethnic.[6] Introduce various types of monuments (e.g., obelisk, flat, upright, mausoleums, and military). Introduce students to the concept of "Boot Hill," where victims of violence were buried with their boots on in the old west.

Epitaphs can be found etched into gravestones as a short text to honor the deceased. Require students to look for various epitaphs or research websites that post memorable sayings, then practice writing their own versions:

Remember friend as you walk by
As you are now so once was I
As I am now you will surely be
Prepare thyself to follow me.[7]

Interest students in learning about what various symbols represent in cemeteries:

- Arch—triumph over death
- Columns—heavenly entrance

- Candle flame—life
- Lyre—recognition of musical talent
- Pineapple—hospitality
- Willow—earthly sorrow
- Flower—premature death[8]

Assign an activity in which students create their own symbols and meanings. What symbol might represent a soldier who died in a war? A leader of a country? A great musician? What symbol would you like to represent you?

Research famous cemeteries around the world: Waverly Cemetery near Sydney, Australia, famous for Victorian and Edwardian monuments; Okunoin, the largest cemetery in Japan noted for unusual headstones; Bonadventure Cemetery in Savannah, Georgia, featured in the novel *Midnight in the Garden of Good and Evil* (Berendt 1999); or Merry Cemetery in Romania, famous for its colorful tombstones. Ask students to find famous cemeteries in their state and discuss what makes the cemetery famous.

As a culminating project, students can volunteer to lead a cemetery tour and discuss with visitors the important gravesites and the history of the town. They may research some of the early settlers buried in the cemetery and create a type of "ghost tour" or "hero's walk" to tell stories of interest about former town members. The website https://www.findagrave.com/ is a good place to find graves or document important gravesites from your community.

For younger students, show the movie *Coco* (directed by Lee Unkrich and Adrian Molina, 2017, Pixar Animation Studios and Walt Disney Pictures) which introduces the celebration of Día de los Muertos (Day of the Dead). You might share other customs to honor the deceased. In Korea during a fall harvest festival, many people visit the graves of their ancestors to pay their respects and clean the graves. Nepal has a Festival of Cows, in which family members who have lost a loved one lead a cow through the center of town. Cows are thought to help guide the deceased to the afterlife. Italians celebrate All Soul's Day by leaving their homes empty in case the deceased want to visit and setting an empty place at the table during meals. Show students that loss is a common thread that unites people.

Show students how to make Papel picado, the Mexican art of cutting tissue paper to make banners. Fold tissue paper and use scissors to cut patterns. The patterns can reflect student personalities or symbols from the celebrations. Hang the folded papers across a length of twine in the classroom.

40. Iconography and Landscape

Content Connections:

Geography, history, civics

Guiding Questions:

- Why do people build monuments/memorials?
- What role do these icons play in society?
- Who do the monuments and memorials represent from our community? Who is not represented?
- Who decides the important people or events to memorialize?
- Who are the heroes of this community? Who are the unsung heroes?

Literature Connections:

Loewen, James. *Lies Across America: What Our Historic Sites Got Wrong.* New York: The New Press. 2019.
Sweeney, Linda Booth. *Monument Maker: Daniel Chester French and the Lincoln Memorial.* Thomaston, ME: Tilbury House Publishers. 2019.
Van Allsburg, Chris. *Ben's Dream.* Boston: Houghton Mifflin. 1982.

Field-based learning is an important tool in social studies instruction. In most communities, memorials, plaques, historical markers, and monuments are erected to record significant events or honor heroes and heroines. These markers could provide historic, economic, political, or geographic insight to community life. These markers are often ignored or taken for granted.

Teachers can make use of the function, importance, location, and meaning—the so-called FILM[9] strategy—to introduce students to the importance of monuments and memorials. The FILM strategy is a great tool to use in the community to teach social studies. Through these activities, students can gain a stronger connection to and an awareness of their community. For each iconographic symbol that students encounter, they should complete the chart in appendix G and answer the following questions:

- *Function*: What purpose is this historic marker serving? What materials were used to construct this marker? Is the marker weathering well? Should it be renovated?
- *Importance*: What event or person does this marker commemorate? When did the event occur? What was happening in this part of the country at the time of that event? Is this event important to everyone in our community? Are there special groups for whom this event is important? Does this event seem important today? Why or why not?
- *Location*: Why is this marker here? Should it be retained? Removed? Revised or recast? Should this site be protected? Was there any opposition?
- *Meaning*: Who erected this marker? When did they erect it? Is that date significant? How? Why did they do so? Was there a program of commemoration when it was first put up? Who is responsible for placing the marker here? For its upkeep? What does the event or person commemorated mean to the community? What does this event or historical person mean for me?

Divide students into teams and assign different areas of the community to each team. Each team is to photograph any monuments/memorials located in their assigned area. Teams will report their findings to the class. Have students investigate any controversy surrounding the monument/memorial. What individuals or groups remained most active in advocating the memorial? Did they encounter any opponents? Use the book *Lies Across America: What Our Historic Sites Got Wrong* (Loewen, 2019) to read about errors on many historical markers. Follow-up activities could include the following:

- Research newspaper articles about such controversies as the Ten Commandments Monument in a Montgomery, Alabama, courthouse.
- Study the artists who designed monuments (e.g., Gutzon Borglum—Mount Rushmore, Frederic Bartholdi—Statue of Liberty, Maya Ying Lin—Vietnam Veterans Memorial).
- Design a memorial or monument to represent an important person or event in the school. Invite community members and caregivers to a showing.
- Examine how diverse peoples in the community are not represented (or an important event from the town history is not represented) and propose a new monument or memorial to City Hall. Conduct background research and make a formal presentation.

- Create a map of the community with symbols for each monument/
  memorial.

For younger students, begin with questions such as "What do Mount
Rushmore, the Statue of Liberty, and the Vietnam Wall all have in common?
What iconography do you know that represents America? What monuments
and memorials do we have in our community?" Read *Ben's Dream* (Van
Allsburg, 1982) to students. This book tells the story of a young boy who
dreams his house floats by monuments of the world. Have students decide
what monuments are represented in the book and mark the location of these
monuments on a map.

41. Community Festivals

Content Connections:

Geography, history, civics, economics

Guiding Questions:

- How do festivals connect to the religion or culture of a community?
- How does geography play into festivals?
- Why are festivals good economic enterprises?
- How do celebrations vary in different cultures?

Literature Connections:

Couvillon, Alice and Elizabeth Moore. *Mimi's First Mardi Gras*. New
    Orleans, LA: Pelican. 1991.
Dawson, Keila. *The King Cake Baby*. New Orleans, LA: Pelican. 2015.
Enderle, Judith Ross. *Something's Happening on Calabash Street*. San Fran-
    cisco, CA: Chronicle Books. 2000.
Fisher, Meaghan. *The Strawberry Festival*. Dayton, OH: Gypsy Publications.
    2015.
Gardner, Alice. *St. Peter's Fiesta*. Gloucester, MA: Alice Gardner Studio. 2017.
Rice, James. *Gaston Goes to Mardi Gras*. New Orleans, LA: Pelican. 1999.

Many communities have festivals based around holidays, religions, or cultures of its members. The festival may include a carnival, fair, parade, music,

food, art, local crafts, or sports event. There are many benefits to hosting a community festival:

- Provides economic value (entrance fees, parking fees, food, beverage, event tickets, souvenirs)
- Attracts tourism
- Celebrates and preserves communal heritage
- Facilitates family and friend reunions
- Develops connections to place
- Promotes positive image of community
- Inspires volunteerism
- Creates a community identity or a sense of community
- Instills community pride
- Initiates marketing and advertising for local businesses or organizations

There can also be challenges to hosting a community festival: financial risks, traffic jams, unexpected harm to visitors, bad weather, or insurance costs. But the benefits definitely outweigh the costs.

Festivals provide a way to offer experiential learning in a fun way. Teachers can use festivals to engage students in the classroom and the community. Begin by looking at famous world festivals.

- *Oktoberfest*—more than six million people around the world attend this festival in Germany. Breweries, beer wagons, and people in folk costumes dominate the celebration.
- *Holi*—ancient Hindu festival in India which celebrates the coming of spring. People smear each other with powdered colors and enjoy fellowship with family and friends.
- *Rio Carnival*—nearly five million people in Brazil take to the streets for a celebration just before the Lent season. Music, dance, food, and parades give people the chance to celebrate before the fasting period begins.
- *Burning Man*—in the Black Rock Desert of Nevada, thousands of bohemians and misfits in crazy costumes burn a huge stick man. The celebration takes place around Labor Day.
- *International Ice and Snow Sculpture Festival*—in northeast China in a place where temperatures can get as low as -31 degree Fahrenheit, a

monthlong celebration occurs with ice sculptures. Over eighteen million visitors come to view the beautiful lighting of these artistic endeavors.

• *Running of the Bulls*—daredevils from around the world come to Pamplona, Spain, to be chased through the streets by bulls. Bullfights, food, and drink round off the festival.

Ask students, "What is the history behind the festival? Why would people from other countries want to attend these festivals? Have celebrations of these festivals translated into other communities?"

Encourage students to create their own community festival by following these guidelines: What is the festival about? Why is it important to celebrate this? When will the festival be held? Where will the festival be held? How will the festival help our community? Who are the target participants for the festival? Will everyone in the community want to celebrate this festival? What do you want the participants to take away from your festival? Of course, the culminating project should be a class participation in a local festival. Have students put together a class-sponsored booth to provide information on their school.

Younger students may already be familiar with the festival of Mardi Gras. The origins of Mardi Gras began in medieval Europe and passed through Rome and Venice in the seventeenth and eighteenth centuries to the French house of the Bourbons. From there the traditional revelry of the Boeuf Gras (fatted bull or ox symbolizing the last meal eaten before the Lent season) or Fatted Calf followed French settlers to the colonies. Yearly parades hosted by "krewes" are prevalent from Brazil to Alabama to New Orleans. The annual extravagance celebrates the overindulgences before the season of Lent begins. Because Mardi Gras (Fat Tuesday) is tied to Easter, the date changes every year.

There are many activities to do with students to prepare a Mardi Gras celebration:

• Share the music of Mardi Gras through songs: "Mardi Gras Mambo," "Go to the Mardi Gras," "Carnival Time."
• Share the history of the king cake and let students taste a king cake. Whoever finds the baby must bring the cake to the next party.
• Share literature with students about Mardi Gras: *Mimi's First Mardi Gras*, *The King Cake Baby*, *Gaston Goes to Mardi Gras*.

- Research the vocabulary of Mardi Gras: carnival (festive season occurring before Lent), doubloon (aluminum, coin-like objects bearing the krewe's insignia on one side and the parade's theme on the reverse), Epiphany (commemorates Magi's visit to the baby Jesus), Twelfth Night (Epiphany Eve), Shrove Tuesday (day before Ash Wednesday), Ash Wednesday (Catholic holy day of prayer and fasting marking the beginning of the Lent season), krewe (generic name for carnival organizations and clubs), king cake (oval, sugared cake with plastic baby doll inside), Laissez Les Bons Temps Rouler (Mardi Gras greeting meaning "Let the Good Times Roll").
- Have students decorate shoeboxes and have a parade of floats. Judges can award prizes to the best floats. Be sure to have a theme for your parade.
- Have a school-wide competition where students can earn points to elect their teacher as "queen" of the carnival.
- Have students create masks to wear on Fat Tuesday. Masks can be made from paper plates or paper bags. Decorate with feathers, glitter, beads, sequins, yarn, felt, ribbon, and markers. Give prizes to the most original mask.
- Have a school Mardi Gras parade and throw beads or candy to students. Have a Mardi Gras ball and elect a court (king, queen, maids, dukes).[10]

42. U.S. Postal Service[11]

Content Connections:

Geography, history

Guiding Questions:

- How do you communicate with people when you cannot communicate face to face?
- How has personal communication changed over the years? How do we communicate today?
- How might a delay of weeks or months affect the information in a written letter of the past?

Literature Connections:

Ahlberg, Janet, and Allan Ahlberg. *The Jolly Postman or Other People's Letters.* New York: Little, Brown and Company. 1986.
Gibbons, Gail. *The Post Office Book: Mail and How It Moves.* New York: Harper Collins. 1982.

Harness, Cheryl. *They're Off! The Story of the Pony Express.* New York:
   Aladdin Books. 2002.
Wells, Rosemary and Tom Wells. *The House in the Mail.* New York: Puffin
   Books. 2004.

The U.S. Postal Service initiated changes in streetlighting and crosswalks, stimulated the development of rural roads and highways, and provided passenger services on railways. The study of the history of the mail service (through foot, air, roads, and rail) and the changes in technology that have affected mail delivery make an interesting topic for social studies. It carved the country into nine-digit zip codes and laid the foundation for the 911 emergency system. Rivers, roads, and rails were designated "postal highways" by acts of Congress. The U.S. airmail paved the way for commercial airlines. The Post Office Department began to build landing fields, towers, beacons, searchlights, and boundary markers across the country. The department also equipped planes with navigational instruments.

Famous postal workers included Abraham Lincoln (president), John Brown (abolitionist), Bing Crosby (singer), Walt Disney (producer), William Faulkner (novelist), Benjamin Franklin (statesman), and Charles Lindbergh (aviator). Students can choose a famous postal worker or a character role to play in a "living museum" in the classroom. Roles may include airmail pilot, postmaster, Pony Express rider, steamboat captain, and walking mailperson. Students will write short narratives that describe their time period and their roles with the mail service. Students will memorize the scripts to be able to tell their stories in a first-person format. Props and costumes will add to the presentations. The museum can be set up to allow for visitors.

Secret correspondence was required by military commanders during the Revolutionary War. Students will be intrigued to gather information on actual spy letters and methods used to write and convey the secret messages. The William L. Clements Library at the University of Michigan hosts an excellent website (http://www2.si.umich.edu/spies/index-people.html) for students with images, stories, and classroom activities on spy letters.

At one time, houses could be ordered through the mail. Ask students to explore the Sears archives (http://www.searsarchives.com/homes/byimage.htm) for images and prices of home kits for sale from 1908 to 1940. Are home kits available for sale today? Are they delivered by the U.S. Postal

Service or private companies? Students can examine Zipkithomes (https://www.zipkithomes.com/), Shelter-Kit (https://www.shelter-kit.com/), and other prefabricated house sites. What are the costs of these home kits? Is there a social stigma attached to the low-quality, mass-produced product? Students could also research housing in their own communities to see if any mail-order homes were purchased.

Connect younger students to pen pals from other countries through https://www.penpalschools.com/. Examine the stamps on the letters and discuss symbols represented. Discuss mail delivery by air, water, and land. Examine the costs of postage and the length of time for delivery of the letters.

NOTES

1. Anthony J. Filipovitch and Talip Ozturk, "Teaching the Social Studies through Your Local Community," *Social Education* 76, no. 2, 2012: 85–87.

2. Adapted from article, Darrell P. Kruger and S. Kay Gandy, "Main Street in the Curriculum: A Fifteen Town Louisiana Case-Study," *Journal of Geography* 105, no 2, 2006: 73–86.

3. Gandy, "Teaching Social Studies on a Shoestring Budget."

4. Kruger and Gandy, "Main Street in the Curriculum."

5. Gandy, "Teaching Social Studies on a Shoestring Budget."

6. Eric Groce, Rachel E. Wilson, and Lisa Poling, "Tomb It May Concern: Visit Your Local Cemetery for a Multidisciplinary (and Economical) Field Trip," *Social Studies and the Young Learner* 25, no. 3, 2013: 13–17.

7. The Epitaph Browser, accessed August 3, 2020, http://www.alsirat.com/epitaphs/.

8. "Symbols Found on Gravestones," The Cemetery Club, accessed August 3, 2020 at http://www.thecemeteryclub.com/symbols.html.

9. Gavin Faichney, "Signs of the Times: Inquiry with Memorial Plaques," *Social Studies and the Young Learner* 13, no. 4, 2001: 22–24.

10. Information collected from Susan Keith, teacher consultant with the Louisiana Geography Education Alliance.

11. Adapted from article, S. Kay Gandy and Cynthia Williams Resor, "Changing Technology and the U.S. Mail," *The Social Studies* 103, no. 6 (2012): 226–232.

Chapter 7

Using Food to Teach Social Studies

Dn. Reson

Social studies textbooks often focus on the political history of a nation and national leaders, yet, a better connection with students could be to introduce the history of ordinary people. One way to teach this effectively is through the use of food in the curriculum. There are many ways to connect food and social studies such as the following:

- Examine cuisines and visit local restaurants to sample dishes studied.
- Explore the influence of geography upon cuisine patterns.

- Study the influence of religious customs such as feasts and fasts (e.g., Advent and Lent).
- Investigate how food affected emigration (e.g., Irish potato famine).
- Delve into diet differences in social orders of the wealthy versus the lower or middle class.[1]

Foods have a central position in our culture. Even our language connects with food, when we speak of ideas such as "food for thought," having someone "eat their words," or not being able to "stomach" unpleasant news.[2] Further exploration of food can include discussing cooking techniques, table manners, ceremonial dishes, origin of appliances or recipes, daily diets, and influences on food choices.

Teachers can make connections with food and history in a variety of ways. The rise of fast foods and takeout can be connected with suburbanization and the entry of women into the workforce. The introduction of canned, frozen, and dehydrated foods can be connected with the end of World War II when companies sought markets for the types of food provided to soldiers. The fast-growing immigrant population in the United States can be connected to the commercialization of Chinese food, Jewish delis, Mexican food, and other unique ethnic dishes.[3]

Another idea to study food would be to look at different categories, such as healthy, natural, prepackaged, or junk.[4] Introduce topics of production, distribution, consumption, and prices of food. Have students investigate when we eat (the number of meals per day, time of day), with whom we eat (same gender, with or without children), how we eat (at a table; on the floor; with chopsticks, silverware, or fingers), the rituals of eating (asking for seconds, belching for appreciation), and what we eat (pork not eaten by Muslims and Orthodox Jews).

Great primary sources to use in the classroom are community cookbooks. Community cookbooks are a collection of recipes compiled to raise money for organizations, churches, and sometimes political causes. Teachers can introduce students to recipe ingredients and their changes over time and across regions. Cookbooks give insight to the life of the everyday person. Community cookbooks also contain information such as the following:

- Advertisements from local businesses
- Stories of local interest

- Quotations and prayers
- Household hints
- Canning and preserving tips
- Changed meanings of words
- Brand-name products featured in recipes[5]

Certainly, a culminating project would be to make a class cookbook. Students will describe traditions associated with recipes, design advertisements for school clubs, and include their favorite quotes or inspirational messages to accompany their favorite recipes.

When using food in the classroom, there are many safety issues to consider. More and more students have allergies to certain types of food, particularly peanuts. At the beginning of a unit involving food, teachers should send home a note to parents with information concerning the food ingredients that will be used. This would be a good time to ask for help in collecting the ingredients. Other considerations would be keeping electrical appliances, glassware, and sharp objects out of the reach of children, letting the children take responsibility for cleanup, and providing children with recipes to take home.[6]

ACTIVITIES FOR USING FOOD TO TEACH SOCIAL STUDIES

43. Earth Models

Content Connections:

Geography

Guiding Questions:

- How can the earth be represented through food?
- How many ways can one food represent the earth?

Literature Connections:

Fuller, Gary and T. M. Reddekopp. *Delicious Geography from Place to Plate*. Lanham, MD: Rowman & Littlefield. 2016.

Getskow, Veronica. *Incredible Edible Geography*. Irvine, CA: Thomas Bros. Maps Educational Foundation. 1998.

The basis of geographic education is location to answer the question "Where is it?" Using fruit is a good way to teach location. Have the students wrap two rubber bands (one vertical and one horizontal) around an orange or a grapefruit and then identify the equator, the prime meridian, and the hemispheres. Introduce terms such as latitude, longitude, north, south, east, west, and parallel. Use a peach or a boiled egg to demonstrate the parts of the earth: core, mantle, crust.

A great way to show the inaccuracies of a flat map is to give students an orange and an orange cutter. Have students draw a map of the world with a permanent marker, then slice the orange around twice and lay out the four pieces side by side. Students can easily see that pieces of the earth are "missing" and that cartographers must "stretch" the land together on a flat map.

Food can even be used to teach map concepts. Give students a type of flat bread, such as Lahvash (soft, unleavened flatbread), and have them draw a map of the school. Inks can be made from milk with food coloring added, and powdered sugar frosting tinted brown with cocoa can be used for map illustrations.[7] Food can also be used to create a variety of environments. Substances that can be used to create sandy environments include raw sugar, rock salt, finely ground oatmeal, or crushed vanilla wafers.[8] River environments can be created with punch, blue tinted water, or whipped cream in a can.[9] Examples of substances to create frozen ice environments include powdered sugar, clear gelatin, white substances, rock salt, and divinity.[10] Cave formations could be created with cupcakes, popovers, cream puffs, or pie crust dough.[11]

Food can be used to create physical characteristics of the earth. For instance, trees could be made with gumdrops and toothpicks (or stick pretzels), and shrubs with vegetables such as broccoli and celery.[12] Depict grass with coconut and green food coloring.[13] A volcano or mountains could be fashioned with soft cookie dough, mountains of whipped cream, or mashed potatoes and gravy.[14]

A favorite with my students was an activity called Luscious Landforms.[15] Bake a rectangle cake and top with white icing. Draw an outline of the United States with red icing. Review landforms and physical features of the United States with students. On index cards, write various landforms and physical features with corresponding ingredients. Students "decorate" the cake in the appropriate places based on the cards they draw:

- Mini chocolate chips—Coast Ranges, Ozark Mountains
- Large chocolate chips—Appalachian Mountains

- Sno-Caps—Rocky Mountains
- Blue icing—Atlantic Ocean, Pacific Ocean, Great Lakes, Gulf of Mexico, Mississippi River
- Green icing—Gulf Coastal Plain, Atlantic Coastal Plain
- Orange icing—Plateaus and Deserts
- Yellow icing—Interior Plain
- Green coconut—prairies
- Red icing—Grand Canyon

Evaluate the finished product. Cut the cake and enjoy eating together.

Use an apple to initiate concern for the protection of the earth's resources. Slice an apple into four equal pieces. Set aside three quarters to represent the oceans of the world. Cut the remaining quarter lengthwise in half. Set aside one piece to represent land inhospitable to people: polar areas, deserts, swamps, mountains. An eighth of the apple represents the area of earth on which the human population lives. Slice the remaining piece into four equal sections. Set aside three pieces to represent land on which food is not grown: cities, highways, schools, parks, factories, poor soil. Peel the remaining piece to represent the tiny bit of earth of which mankind depends to grow its food. Ask the students to identify what fraction of the earth is remaining (1/32) and tell why we should protect the earth's resources.[16]

Introduce younger students to nonrenewable resources through an activity with cookies about mining. Give each student a toothpick, paper towel, and chocolate chip cookie. Explain to students that the cookies represent the earth and the chips represent coal that they will be mining. With the toothpicks, have students carefully remove each chip. The cookie should stay flat on the paper towel. Ask students if they experienced any difficulties (typically the cookie falls to pieces). Then ask students to "reclaim" the land using the toothpicks. Discuss the difficulties that coal mining companies face with land management.[17]

44. Origins of Food and Appliances

Content Connections:

Geography, history, economics

Guiding Questions:

- How are foods alike around the world?
- What are some celebratory uses of food?

Literature Connections:

Barrett, Judi. *Cloudy with a Chance of Meatballs.* New York: Atheneum Books for Young Readers. 1982.

Dooley, Norah. *Everybody Cooks Rice.* Minneapolis, MN: Carolrhoda Picture Books.1991.

Lopez-Alt, J. Kenji. *Every Night Is Pizza Night.* New York: Norton Young Readers. 2020.

Priceman, Marjorie. *How to Make an Apple Pie and See the World.* Decorah, IA: Dragonfly Books. 1996.

Some activities that students can do with food include researching the origin of food and the regions they come from. For example, students will guess that the word "pizza" is the Italian word for pie. U.S. soldiers brought it back to America from Italy at the end of World War II. Pizza seems to be the number one food choice for teenagers. Where did it come from? Why is it so popular? In 2019, there were nearly 77,000 pizzerias in the United States.[18] Students could look at various types of pizza styles offered: Chicago, Sicilian, Neapolitan, California, deep-dish, stuffed, thin crust, pan. Have a taste test with pizza from a restaurant, from a do-it-yourself kit, and frozen pizza. Ask students to list all their favorite toppings, then find out where their ingredients were produced.

Present interesting facts about foods to students that could lead to research on food growing regions and ask questions, such as "What kinds of dumplings are eaten around the world (Chinese wonton, Italian ravioli, Indian modak, Jewish kreplach, Russian pelmeni, Swedish pitepalt, and Polish pierogi)? What are dumplings filled with (meat, cheese, vegetables)? What are dumplings made from (potatoes, bread, rice, dough)? How can food be used to characterize a region?"[19]

Another tie to food origins would be to explain that bread is used across cultures to celebrate religious or civil ceremonies, as a staple food item, and often as a sign of friendship and sharing. One way to connect students with other cultures is to introduce the similarities of bread types across the world. The English and American pancake can be compared with French crepes, Mexican tortillas, Italian frittella, Hungarian palacintas, and Russian blini.[20]

The Amish friendship bread starter was handed down from mother to daughter through many generations. Once you made the bread, you passed along a sample of the bread and the starter to friends. These friends then make the bread and pass along to their friends. Appendix H has the Amish Friendship Bread recipe shared with me many years ago from one of my friends. Have students make the bread starter and share with other classes in the school.

The origin of Johnny Cakes connects Native Americans to colonial settlers. One story suggests that Johnny Cakes originally were called "journey cakes," because they were so often taken and eaten on long journeys. A common Indian corn recipe consisted of cornmeal and water wrapped in a leaf and left to bake. The cakes were often eaten with butter, maple syrup, or stew gravy. Have students trace the movement of corn and corn recipes throughout North America, then share with students the Johnny Cake Recipe in appendix I.

Louisiana is noted for Cajun cuisine and makes an interesting tableau for taste and research. Ask students to research the ingredients from Cajun gumbo that came from other cultures: African vegetable "okra," Choctaw spice "file powder," French base "roux," German meat "andouille sausage." Even jambalaya, a Cajun rice dish, was based on the Spanish "paella." Tabasco Sauce, also made in Louisiana, is credited to Edmund McIlhenny, a wealthy plantation owner who lost everything in the Civil War except his crop of hot peppers. The world-famous sauce was created with vinegar, salt, and chopped peppers.[21] Some sources credit Maunsel White as discovering the peppers and making a sauce that inspired McIlhenny. Encourage students to research both inventors and debate the issue.

Hamburger was originally called hamburger steak and named after Hamburg, Germany. Frankfurters were named after the town of Frankfurt, Germany. They were also known as hot dog, wiener, and frank. This meat was made from beef, pork, veal, chicken, or turkey. An American vendor in 1900 supposedly called them "hot dachshund sausages" because they resembled the dog.[22] Assign students to research other food origins and present their findings in class.

The origins of appliances and helpful kitchen tools (can openers, scrubber pads, sandwich bags) are another area of interest to students. Food in early days was prepared over an open hearth, or perhaps a woodburning or coal-heated stove. Fruits and vegetables were typically dried or preserved. Use an investigative tool to challenge students to research and answer questions that led to the inventions of appliances, such as "What was the problem? Why was it a problem? What attempts were made to solve the problem?"[23]

Students may be delighted to find out that many inventions happened by error or accident. You may also have students compare appliances in the past to the present. For example, the popular Instant Pot is a modern-day pressure cooker. Students may note that appliances today are more affordable, reliable, and energy efficient.

For younger students, play a game called Where in the World Does this Food Come From? Have a world map on the wall and picture cards of various foods. Students can use yarn to match the food to the country. Some examples include shepherd's pie—UK; paella—Spain; sushi—Japan; tacos—Mexico; curry—India. Introduce the term "comfort food." Ask students, "What is that one special food that you like when you feel sad or ill?" For some people, the food is sweet, like ice cream or chocolate. Others might prefer food like chicken soup or macaroni and cheese. Ask students, "What about this food makes you feel better?"

45. Food and Literature

Content Connections:

Geography, economics

Guiding Questions:

- Where does our food come from?
- What food is produced in our area?

Literature Connections:

Brown, Marcia. *Stone Soup*. New York: Aladdin Picture Books. 1997.
Butterworth, Chris. *How Did that Get in My Lunchbox? The Story of Food*. Somerville, MA: Candlewick. 2011.
Carle, Eric. *Pancakes, Pancakes*. New York: Simon & Schuster Books for Young Readers. 1992.
Dooley, Norah. *Everybody Cooks Rice*. Minneapolis, MN: Carolrhoda Picture Books. 1991.
Krull, Kathleen. *Supermarket*. New York: Holiday House. 2001.
Morris, Ann. *Bread, Bread, Bread*. New York: HarperCollins. 1989.
McClure, Nikki. *To Market, To Market*. New York: Harry N. Abrams. 2011.

Muth, John J. *Stone Soup*. New York: Scholastic Press. 2003
Wilder, Laura Ingalls. *Little House on the Prairie*. HarperCollins. 2008.

Literature has always integrated well with social studies, but teachers can easily make the food connection too, such as baking bread when reading about the westward movement in the *Little House on the Prairie* (Wilder, 2008) books.

A field trip to the supermarket to buy ingredients for a recipe would give students the opportunity to examine labels for places that food comes from. An alternative might be to read books about food: *Supermarket* (Krull, 2001), which describes how food gets from farm to shelf; *How Did that Get in My Lunchbox? The Story of Food* (Butterworth, 2011), which focuses on processes to make bread, pick fruit, and make chocolate; or *To Market, To Market* (McClure, 2011), which gives information about how each food in the market is produced or grown. Ask the students to determine where the food in the cafeteria served for lunch today came from.

Since bread and rice are staple ingredients of most ethnic groups, two additional books to include in the classroom are *Bread, Bread, Bread* (Morris 1989) and *Everybody Cooks Rice* (Dooley, 1991). Plan a bread-tasting day and include baguette (France), pita (Israel), pretzel (Germany), tortilla (Mexico), or naan (India). Instruct students to map wheat growing regions in central United States, Argentina, central Canada, northwest India, Australia, southern Russia, north central China, Mediterranean region, and Danube River region.[24]

For younger students, there are children's books that relate to human/environment relationships and naturally lend themselves to cooking in the classroom. In *Pancakes, Pancakes* (Carle, 1992), Jack's mother needs flour from the mill, an egg from the hen, milk from the cow, and firewood for the stove to make pancakes. Included within the story is a page with pictures of all the ingredients, almost like a photo recipe. Discuss with students how humans depend on the environment for food. Ask students, how do we get ingredients today to make pancakes?

Stone Soup (Brown, 1997), a children's book based on an old French tale, regales the story of three traveling soldiers who trick some miserly villagers into giving up their hordes of vegetables and making a community pot of soup. A newer version of the story (Muth, 2003) changes the soldiers to three traveling monks who enlighten villagers in China about the happiness of sharing. Students will be delighted to make a pot of soup in the classroom that starts with a smooth, washed stone from the playground, as they write their own version of the story using cultural elements.

46. Cooking and Recipes

Content Connections:

Geography, history, economics

Guiding Questions:

- What influences the ingredients of a recipe?
- What kinds of recipes are popular in our area?

Literature Connections:

Cannon, Poppy. *The Can-Opener Cookbook*. New York: Thomas Crowell. 1955.

Rockwell, Thomas. *How to Eat Fried Worms*. New York: Scholastic, Inc. 2019.

Saeed, Aisha. *Bilal Cooks Daal*. New York: Simon & Schuster Books for Young Readers. 2019.

Soto, Gary. *Too Many Tamales*. London: Puffin Books. 1996.

Magazines today inevitably publish recipes, whether following a theme (summer bar-b-que), or sharing a favorite recipe of a celebrity, or promoting a product (e.g., Baker's Chocolate, Knox Gelatin). Some recipes are for quick meals, while others include unusual ingredients and take a lot of time. Cookbooks abound in bookstores, at gift shops, or at home. The role of women and cooking has flexed over the years. Poppy Cannon introduced *The Can-Opener Cookbook* (1955) for busy people in need of quick gourmet meals straight out of a can, box, or bag. Julia Child, on the other hand, gave women the confidence to cook meals from scratch through her television show and cookbooks. Encourage students to research and find out, "Who was Betty Crocker? Who was Duncan Hines? How did they change the way people cooked?"

Ask students to look for recipes that feature products (e.g., Royal Baking Powder) and determine if the brand products are needed specifically, and if so, why. Students can also examine cookbooks from the past and answer questions such as the following:

• Are the recipes for these dishes commonly prepared today?
• Could you follow this recipe and prepare this food? Why or why not?
• What equipment or technology is required to prepare this food?
• Circle unfamiliar ingredients or words (e.g., gill, syllabub).[25]

Cookbook measurements in the past signified real teaspoons and cups. There was no standardized system.[26] At one time eggs were used as a measurement system. For example, to bake a cake, ten eggs defined the amount of sugar to be used, six eggs defined the amount of flour.[27] Ask students, "How much is a 'pinch' of salt? How much is a 'dash' of salt?" Other measurements to research would be "tad," "smidgen," "drop," "pat," and "shake." Examine recipes from the past and from today. Do these terms still apply? Why or why not?

Students will enjoy researching exotic foods eaten by wealthy people in the past. Some examples include brains of peacocks, tongues of flamingos, vegetables mixed with gold, rice and fish mixed with pearls.[28] Ask students, "Why didn't peasants eat these foods? What did they eat?" Introduce students to unusual foods eaten by various cultures around the world: fried tarantulas in Cambodia, live octopus in Korea, snake wine in Vietnam, stuffed camel in the Persian Gulf region, birds nest soup in China. There are television shows produced that feature unusual cuisine (e.g., "Bizarre Foods with Andrew Zimmern") so that students can review film of these exotic dishes. Require students to come up with their own unusual food choices.

You may ask students, "Are there places where food is not readily available? What causes a food shortage?" You might discuss drought, early frost, man-made destruction of the environment, and even, a pandemic. Can you substitute ingredients in a recipe? Many cookbooks have ideas for substitutions: one square of chocolate can be substituted with three or four tablespoons of cocoa plus one tablespoon butter; one cup whole milk can be substituted with half cup evaporated milk plus half cup water; half cup brown sugar can be substituted with two tablespoons molasses in half cup granulated sugar.[29] Introduce students to rationing that occurred during the World Wars.

For younger students, you might share the book *How to Eat Fried Worms* (Rockwell, 2019). Crumble Oreo cookies in a cup and add gummy worms for a special treat afterward. Ask students, "What do you think worms might taste like?" The Travel Channel website has photos of thirteen places in the United States to taste bug-based delicacies. https://www.travelchannel.com/shows /bizarre-foods/photos/13-places-in-the-u-s-to-try-bug-based-delicacies. Ask students, "Why would someone want to eat a bug?"

NOTES

1. Bertram M. Gordon, "Food and History," *The Social Studies* 65 no. 5, (1973): 204–207, DOI: 10.1080/00220973.1943.11019347.

2. Elizabeth Cooper, "Something to Sink Their Teeth Into: Teaching Culture through Food," *Transformations* 23, no. 2 (2013): 92–105, 183.

3. Michael P. Marino and Margaret S. Crocco, "Pizza: Teaching US History through Food and Place," *The Social Studies* 106, no. 4, (2015): 149–158, DOI: 10.1080/00377996.2015.1020354.

4. Cynthia Williams Resor, *Investigating Family, Food, and Housing Themes in Social Studies* (New York: Rowman & Littlefield, 2017): 67.

5. Cynthia Williams Resor, "Using Community Cookbooks as Primary Sources," *Social Education* 75, no. 1 (2011): 30–35.

6. Paula Nunez and Carolyn Brugmann, "Dos and Don'ts for Cooking in the Classroom," paper presentation at the Louisiana Council for the Social Studies conference in Lafayette, LA, 1999.

7. Veronica Getskow, *Incredible Edible Geography* (Irvine, CA: Thomas Bros. Maps Educational Foundation, 1998): 11.

8. Getskow, *Incredible Edible Geography*, 43.

9. Getskow, *Incredible Edible Geography*, 39.

10. Getskow, *Incredible Edible Geography*, 27.

11. Getskow, *Incredible Edible Geography*, 19.

12. Getskow, *Incredible Edible Geography*, 23.

13. Getskow, *Incredible Edible Geography*, 25.

14. Getskow, *Incredible Edible Geography*, 49.

15. Adapted from lesson "Luscious Landforms," by Paula Nunez, Teacher Consultant with the Louisiana Geography Education Alliance.

16. Adapted from lesson "Earth: the Apple of Our Eye," Population Connection, accessed May 12, 2020, https://populationeducation.org/wp-content/uploads/2017/10 /earth_the_apple_of_our_eye_elem.pdf.

17. Adapted from lesson "Mining for Chocolate," Population Connection, accessed May 12, 2020, https://populationeducation.org/sites/default/files/mining-for -chocolate.pdf.

18. Akila McConnell, "11 Fast Facts about the History of Pizza." ThoughtCo, accessed at April 13, 2020, https://www.thoughtco.com/history-of-pizza-1329091.

19. Adapted from lesson "How Old Is Food?" presented by Ava Pugh and JoAnne Welch at the Louisiana Council for the Social Studies conference in Lafayette, LA (1999).

20. Efi Psilaki, "Sharing Cultures through Food: Teaching in a Multicultural University Classroom," *Transformations: The Journal of Inclusive Scholarship and Pedagogy* 23, no. 2 (2012): 130–140.

21. Barbara A. Hatcher, "Who's in the Kitchen with Dinah? History!," *The Social Studies* 81, no. 3 (1990): 101–105.

22. Pugh and Welch, "How Old Is Food?"

23. Hatcher, "Who's in the Kitchen with Dinah?"

24. Getskow, *Incredible Edible Geography*, 52.

25. Resor, *Investigating Family, Food, and Housing Themes in Social Studies*, 102.

26. Resor, "Using Community Cookbooks as Primary Sources," 30–35.

27. Hilde Lee, "Standardized Measurements Weren't on the Menu Until Late 19th Century," *The Daily Progress*, published October 3, 2017, accessed at https://www .dailyprogress.com/entertainment/lifestyles/hilde-lee-standardized-measurements -werent-on-the-menu-until-late-19th-century/article_8a66f824-a49b-11e7-b7c4 -6717a2a24965.html.

28. Resor, *Investigating Family, Food, and Housing Themes in Social Studies*, 73.

29. Ingredient substitutions from *A Literary Feast: A Collection of Recipes from Northwest Regional Libraries* (Kearney, NE: Morris Press Cookbooks, 2011): 132.

Chapter 8

Using Experiential Learning to Teach Social Studies

Simulations/Role Play/Debate/Scenarios

With experiential learning, students take on different roles and interact in diverse settings. A "simulation" might involve a familiar or realistic situation in which students take roles in a simulated world. The teacher controls the parameter of the world in which the students interact, make decisions, and solve problems. For example, students may play the roles of townspeople who meet to discuss trade with Native Americans or play the roles of an economic advisory panel to the president to discuss military spending.

Simulation allows free choice of actions and speech, as there is no script to follow.

Before introducing a simulation to students, you need to spend some time teaching students how to role-play a character. Give students a simple scenario, such as "you've just won the lottery," or "you've discovered a long-lost relative," or "you are a new student in a class." You may set up a situation, such as a mock interview. Allow students time to get used to playing a different person.

Role play allows students the opportunity to see a problem or issue from a different perspective. There are no costumes or scripts and students have minimal time to plan what they will do or say. Students can practice foreign language skills, conduct parent/child interactions, or take on the role of a government leader. You might allow improvisation, as students take on the role of a sitting president and share what they might say to past presidents. Students may even video themselves as they show the steps to paint a room, give a speech, or play a musical instrument.

In leading up to the simulation game, you might try introducing scenarios. In a scenario, students will react to one situation posed by the teacher. For example, tell students that they are a group of people forced to follow the religious code of the area. What would they do? Would they rebel and chance being arrested? Would they make do and follow the system? Would they try to overthrow the government? Put students into groups and allow them to make and justify their choice. Then teach students about a time in history when a group of people had to make this same type of choice.

Case studies are closely related to scenarios and often involve situations from an actual case. Case studies typically include some question or problem that needs to be solved, a description of the problem's context, and supporting data. You might start with a problem like, "How can we improve school attendance?" Discuss with students what they will need to research in order to come up with a viable answer. Students can work in small groups or individually to solve the case study. Make sure the problem is relevant to the students' lives and give them enough context to feel confident in their solutions. Once you have practiced with role play, case studies, and scenario assignments, you are ready to begin a simulation game in which students are immersed in a real-world environment to make decisions.

The first step for the simulation game is to set up the background for the simulation. Students cannot make decisions about or act out the role of a soldier in a war or a U.N. delegate if they have no context about the situation. Students need this information in order to be successful in their roles. You can assign roles or allow students to choose their roles. Once students begin the simulation, do not interrupt them or give them advice. Allow them to think critically and make their own choices. To enhance the fun for students, have a variety of costumes, wigs, hats, and props available. If the characters are assigned ahead of time, students can bring their own prop or make their own costume.

Debriefing the activity is essential for students to have the opportunity to analyze their actions, discuss what happened, and gain a deeper understanding from the experience. Some questions to ask may include the following:

- What did you learn from this experience?
- How did you feel during each of the roles?
- How was this simulation similar to the real events that occurred? How was it different?
- What do you think you could have done differently? Why?
- How can you improve next time?
- Did the simulation help you better understand the events in history?[1]

Simulations take a lot of time and preparation. Students may think they are just playing a game, so at times you may need to remind them of the educational purpose of the activity. It may be easy to trivialize people or events through simulations, so know what your students can handle sensitively. Be sure that your students thoroughly understand what is expected of them and hold students accountable for their participation.

Debate is another experiential learning activity that would allow for collaborative work with students. Working in pairs or groups, students will be asked to take one of two positions or perspectives to debate a topic. Students need to spend at least a week investigating their issue and preparing their statements. Show videos of debates so that students see the mechanics of a good debate or invite local debate team members to visit the classroom. The teacher can serve as the moderator (or choose an unbiased guest) to help each side honor the time limits, stay on subject, and show respect for each other.

The audience or moderator will score each team on criteria such as delivery, strength of argument, relevance, and enthusiasm. You can score by individual or team (or both). Debate is a strong tool for teaching students teamwork, respect for other viewpoints, research, speaking, and listening skills.[2]

ACTIVITIES USING EXPERIENTIAL
LEARNING TO TEACH SOCIAL STUDIES

47. Mock Trials

Content Connections:

Civics

Guiding Questions:

- Who are the participants in a trial?
- How does the court system work?

Literature Connections:

Aronfeld, Spencer M. *Sara Rose, Kid Lawyer*. Bloomington, IN: Author-House. 2010.
Matsuoka, Mei. *The Three Little Pigs*. Bath, England: Parragon Books. 2018.
Scieszka, Jon. *The True Story of the 3 Little Pigs*. London: Puffin Books. 1996.

Familiar stories provide the background and setting for hosting fun mock trials in the classroom. Interesting cases include Witch versus Hansel and Gretel (trespassing), Whoville versus Grinch (stealing Christmas), or Munchkins versus Dorothy (murder of the wicked witch). By simulating investigations and trials, students are challenged to use critical thinking, debate, speaking, and drama skills.

One of the most popular mock trials is Goldilocks versus The Three Bears. A curious little girl named Goldilocks broke into the peaceful home of Mama Bear, Papa Bear, and Baby Bear. While there, she sampled food that was prepared for the family, broke a chair, and vandalized the Bears' bedroom. A police officer noticed a broken window in front of the Bears' cottage and stopped to check on the Bear family. Goldilocks almost knocked the officer down as she tried to flee the scene. Goldilocks was arrested and charged with breaking and entering and destruction of personal property. Students must decide if Goldilocks is guilty as charged or simply curious and innocent of wrongdoing.

Begin by dividing students into their roles: prosecuting team, defense team, judge, jury, defendants, witnesses, clerk of court, and bailiff. Students gather evidence, develop characters, and plan strategies. At the end of the trial preparation, each group must submit a summary report of the group's preparations. Copies of all sworn statements, summary reports, and lists of evidence must be available to be shared with other groups.

The judge and jury members must know about trial procedures, evaluating evidence, and making fair decisions. The clerk of court and bailiff must understand courtroom procedures and assist the court in the formality of the proceedings. The prosecution and defense attorneys must know all facts of the case and must prepare persuasive arguments to present to the court. One attorney should prepare an opening statement, while a different lawyer will prepare a closing statement. The attorneys must also develop questions that they will ask the defense and prosecution witnesses and decide which attorney will examine and cross-examine witnesses. The judge explains to the jury appropriate rules of law that it is to be considered in weighing the evidence. As a rule, the prosecution must meet the burden of proof in order to prevail.

For younger students, read *The Three Little Pigs*, which tells the story from the pigs' perspectives, and *The True Story of the Three Little Pigs*, which tells the story from the wolf's perspective. After reading both books, then have the students vote on who they think is telling the truth: the wolf or the pigs.

With the younger students, set up the beginnings of a mock trial of the Wolf versus The Three Pigs. Divide students into three groups: prosecuting team, defense team, and news team. Each team gets three minutes to plan their statements. The news team introduces the story of what happened. A reporter from the field can interview possible witnesses. The prosecuting team and defense team give opening statements to jurors in preparation for a trial. After the presentations, you can discuss with students what might happen next.

48. World on a String[3]

Content Connections:

Geography, economics

Guiding Questions:

- How are countries around the world interconnected?
- Why do countries need to import and export goods?

Literature Connections:

Adler, David A. *Prices, Prices, Prices: Why They Go Up and Down*. New York: Holiday House. 2016.

Brezina, Corona. *How Imports and Exports Work*. New York: Rosen Publishing Group. 2011.

Bullard, Lisa. *Lily Learns about Wants and Needs*. Minneapolis, MN: Cloverleaf Books. 2013.

Loewen, Nancy. *Lemons and Lemonade: A Book about Supply and Demand*. Bloomington, MN: Picture Window Books. 2005.

Give each student a card with a country name and exports to a different country. The CIA World Factbook (https://www.cia.gov/library/publications /the-world-factbook/) has a list of countries and exports students can use to find information for export cards. Put students in a large circle and have each student hold a card. Make sure the card numbers are not consecutive in the circle. The first student will read the card and throw a ball of twine to the trading partner. For example, the card may say, "I am the United States and I export corn to Russia." The student will keep the end of string and throw the ball of twine to student holding Russia card. The game continues until a web is made. The pattern made could represent cargo shipping and air routes throughout the world. Tell students, if your export affects automotive industry, tug on the string. If your export affects food industry, tug on the string. If your export affects the clothing industry, tug on the string. Who feels a tug? Why?

Discuss various problems that might impede the trading process, such as pirates in the oceans, government regulations, natural disasters, or trade disputes. Tell students, a drought in Europe has destroyed crops and animals. If your country receives an export from Europe, tug on the string. Who felt the tug? How will the drought affect your country?

For younger students, examine each other's clothing labels to see where items were made. Put stickers on a map as students discover each country. Ask students, what country has the most stickers? How do you think the clothing items got to our state? What types of transportation might be used? Share with students a product, such as a pencil, and discuss where each piece of the pencil comes from: rubber for the eraser—Thailand and Malaysia; wood—Sweden and South Africa; graphite (lead)—Brazil and Mexico; yellow paint—Kazakhstan and Estonia; metal that holds eraser to pencil—China and Mozambique.[4]

49. Take a Stand[5]

Content Connections:

Civics

Guiding Questions:

- Why is it important to listen to the opinions of others?
- Why is it important to "take a stand"?

Literature Connections:

Krasner, Barbara. *Goldie Takes a Stand: Golda Meir's First Crusade.* Minneapolis, MN: Kar-Ben Publishing. 2014.

Rinker, Jess. *Gloria Takes a Stands: How Gloria Steinem Listened, Wrote and Changed the World.* London: Bloomsbury Children's Books. 2019.

Tucker, Zoe. *Greta and the Giants: Inspired by Greta Thunberg's Stand to Save the World.* London: Frances Lincoln Children's Books. 2019.

This activity is an opportunity for students to think through issues and weigh the opinions of others. Post signs around the room labeled strongly agree, agree, disagree, and strongly disagree. As you read statements to students, have them "take a stand" by one of the signs and defend their stance. Tell students there can be no "neutral" stances. Some sample statements include the following:

- There should be a law to require everyone to recycle.
- Creating jobs is more important than preserving the environment.
- It is ok to cut down the rainforest to have land for living and growing food.
- Because we live in one of the richest nations of the world, we should welcome all those from other nations who wish to live here.

To keep students on task, ask students to paraphrase the opinions offered by others before stating their own opinion. You may want to give students a list of the statements ahead of time so that they may think about their responses. Ask students if their opinion has changed after listening to statements by their classmates.

For younger students, have them agree, disagree, or stand neutral in the middle if they are not sure about their beliefs. Start with a story and then ask students if they agreed or disagreed with a character's choice and why. Instead of standing on one side of the room or the other, you may have students place sticky notes on an "agree" or "disagree" poster.

50. Town Simulation[6]

Content Connections:

Geography, history, civics, economics

Guiding Questions:

• Why is it important that citizens have a voice in community actions?
• How can you have a voice in your community?

Literature Connections:

Grote, JoAnn A. *Kate and the Spies: The American Revolution (1775)*. Uhrichsville, OH: Barbour Books. 2004.

Miloszewski, Nathan. *Patriots and Loyalists*. New York: PowerKids Press. 2019.

Minniti, Jackie. *One Small Spark*. Tampa Bay, FL: Anaiah Press. 2018.

Nelson, Bruce and Brent Colley. *The Revolution Comes to Redding: Jonas Fairchild's Journal 1778-1779*. Amazon.com Services LLC. 2019.

Turner, Ann. *Love Thy Neighbor: The Tory Diary of Prudence Emerson*. New York: Scholastic, Inc. 2003.

Winters, Kay. *Colonial Voices: Hear Them Speak: The Outbreak of the Boston Tea Party Told from Multiple Points of View!* London: Puffin Books. 2015.

Divide students into Patriots, Loyalists, and Neutral citizens of a town in the 1770s that must decide whom to support in the Revolutionary War—the new colonies or the monarchy in England (try to have an equal number for each side and some neutral citizens). In this emergency town meeting, citizens must each speak about their views and experiences before the vote is taken. Most are rural farmers or small businessmen with families. Many members in each family have opposing views. Every man, woman, and child will get a vote on this important issue. Students must create a costume or bring an artifact to represent their character and be prepared to talk from the viewpoint of their character. For example, the preacher may bring a Bible and read a scripture that is against war.

Typical characters include the following:

- Tavern owner who fought in French and Indian War. The wife works at the tavern and shares the views of her husband. The older son attends college and has different views from the family. The younger son is neutral and must be convinced to take a side.
- Preacher who is paid in food and money that the townspeople give him. Typically, he sides with the king.
- Wealthy nobleman whose support comes solely from the king.
- Banker who only honors Loyalist money.
- Former college professor who can see both sides.
- Widow of a soldier.
- Orphan who does not really understand the issues.
- General of the local regiment.
- Patriot recruiter and Loyalist recruiter who try to stir up the people.
- Schoolteacher who is undecided on the issues.
- Native American who scouts for the local townspeople.
- Farmer who lives on the outskirts of town.
- Butcher who prefers a cash business and doesn't care which side pays.

The moderator will welcome the townspeople to this important meeting and thank them for attending. Each person will stand up and introduce him/herself and will be allowed two minutes maximum to speak their viewpoint. The moderator will facilitate the back and forth presentations of speakers. When all characters have spoken, the town moderator takes a simple majority roll call vote to determine the allegiance of the town.

To debrief the simulation, ask students how they felt in their roles. Have students determine what reasoning points from various characters were useful to the meeting. Discuss with students how their vote might be different if they had to vote today on whether or not to go to war. Remind students of ways they can have a voice in their own community: voting, signing petitions, attendance at public events (e.g., city council meeting), writing letters to leaders, participating in a protest, and partnering with nonprofit organizations.

Simulations for younger students would be simpler scenarios that connect to ideas they are familiar with. Assign students roles as principal, teacher, librarian, cafeteria worker, and custodian welcoming students to a new school. Rather than whole class, try small group simulations. Students could also act out scenarios where someone needed aid from a community helper: police officer, firefighter, plumber, crossing guard, veterinarian, or mechanic.

NOTES

1. Heather LeBlanc. "Free Simulation: 7 Ways to Step Away from the Lecture Podium and Revitalize Your Social Studies Classroom." Blog post at Brainy Apples, accessed August 1, 2020, https://www.brainyapples.com/2018/02/06/simulationsinss/.

2. Michael D. Evans, "Using Classroom Debates as a Learning Tool," *Social Education* 57, no. 7 (1993): 370.

3. Adapted from a lesson "The World on a String," by Germaine Wagner, Professional Development Coordinator Wyoming Geographic Alliance, accessed August 29, 2020, http://www.uwyo.edu/wga/_files/2012-2013%20lesson%20plans/world_on_string.pdf.

4. From lesson "Geography of a Pencil," National Geographic, accessed October 13, 2020 at https://www.nationalgeographic.org/activity/geography-of-a-pencil/.

5. Adapted from lesson "Take a Stand," Population Education, accessed August 30, 2020 https://populationeducation.org/wp-content/uploads/2017/10/take_a_stand.pdf.

6. Adapted from simulation accessed August 28, 2020, http://inquiryunlimited.org/lit/townsim/simmtg.html.

Conclusion

Learning social studies allows students to gain knowledge and understanding of the past, an appreciation of cultural differences, and a connection and awareness of the world around us. It is critical that we create students who are willing to participate in the democratic process by making informed decisions, who are open and accepting of other people and perspectives, and who care about the world. Teachers are the guides who provide context to everyday life as they prepare students for the future.

The eight themes and fifty activities in this book are tied to real-world learning, yet there are many more possibilities for teaching social studies. As a classroom teacher, I used social studies topics as the main theme of my instruction and built all the other subject areas around it. For example, I used the theme of the election process to plan a six-week unit during a presidential election year. For reading and spelling, I used the book *The Kid Who Ran for President* (Gutman, 2012). For science, we looked at the candidates' stances on various issues such as, climate change. For history, we researched voting rights. For math, we looked at campaign budgets and electoral votes. For geography, we mapped votes across the United States during the election.

To accompany the election process unit, I divided the students into Republicans and Democrats. They each nominated a candidate to run for class president. Each party wrote campaign slogans and speeches, designed campaign songs and posters, and participated in debates. Each class member was assigned a state so that the electoral votes were used to choose the final winner. My class president then chose officers to serve with him. Students were active participants in learning social studies in meaningful ways.

Civics, geography, economics, and history are not meant to be taught in isolation, any more than social studies is meant to be taught in isolation. It does not matter if you have an outdated social studies textbook, as this is just one resource to use when you teach. The community, primary sources, music, food, visual media, the environment, literature, and simulations are readily available for teachers, as well as many more real-world connections. It is my hope that this book will inspire you to search your own environment and find interesting and relevant connections for your students.

Appendix A

Salt Dough Recipe for Making Tiles

Two cups flour
One cup salt
One cup water
Two tablespoons vegetable oil
Food coloring or acrylic paint[1]

In a large bowl, mix flour and salt. Add the oil, and then slowly add the water and stir until you get a nice clay consistency. If you want the dough to be different colors, separate the dough into portions and put them in a bowl. Add a couple of drops of food coloring to each portion and mix well with a spoon. Once completely mixed, make the dough into the desired shapes.

Bake in a 250 degree Fahrenheit oven for approximately one hour, although the timing will vary depending on how thick your creations are. Bake it long enough for the dough to harden but not start to burn. The dough can be air-dried for forty-eight to seventy-two hours if you do not have access to an oven.

Use acrylic paint to design tile patterns.

NOTE

1. Recipe from "How to Make Clay with Flour," The Spruce Crafts, accessed August 20, 2020, https://www.thesprucecrafts.com/oven-flour-clay-recipe-1250343.

Appendix B

The Little Red Hen Operetta
Based on the Original Story
by S. Kay Gandy

Scenery: a barnyard

Props: bundle of wheat, sickle, sack of flour, wheelbarrow, loaf of bread

Characters: Mother Hen, Duck, Cat, Dog, Chicks, Chorus

Chorus sings "This is the Story" to introduce the characters.

Curtain opens on the barnyard scene. Mother Hen is clucking and scratching in the yard and finds a grain of wheat. Duck, cat, and dog are sleeping.

Mother Hen: (excitedly) Look what I found! If this wheat were planted, it would grow into more wheat. Then it could be ground into flour and made into bread. Who will help me plant this wheat?

Duck: (yawning) Not I.

Cat: (sleepily) Not I.

Dog: (uncaringly) Not I.

Chorus sings "Not I."

Mother Hen: Very well then, I will.

Chorus sings first verse of "Work Song" as Mother Hen plants the wheat. Wheat is made to grow and multiply.

Mother Hen: Look how tall and golden my wheat has grown! Who will help me cut the wheat?

131

Duck: Not I.

Cat: Not I.

Dog: Not I.

Chorus sings "Not I."

Mother Hen: Very well then, I will.

Chorus sings second verse of "Work Song" as Mother Hen cuts the wheat with the sickle.

Mother Hen: Look at this nice bundle of wheat. Who will help me thresh the wheat?

Duck, cat, and dog are playing a game.

Duck: Not I.

Cat: Not I.

Dog: Not I.

Chorus sings "Not I."

Mother Hen: Very well then, I will.

Chorus sings third verse of "Work Song" as Mother Hen threshes the wheat and places it in the wheelbarrow.

Mother Hen: Will anyone help me take the wheat to the mill and have it ground into flour?

Duck: Not I.

Cat: Not I.

Dog: Not I.

Chorus sings "Not I."

Mother Hen: Very well then, I will.

Chorus sings fourth verse of "Work Song" as Mother Hen pushes the wheelbarrow offstage and returns with a sack of flour.

Mother Hen: Who will help me make this flour into bread?

Duck, cat, and dog are lazily lounging around.

Duck: Not I.

Cat: Not I.

Dog: Not I.

Chorus sings "Not I."

Mother Hen: Very well then, I will.

Chorus sings fifth verse of "Work Song" as Mother Hen takes flour offstage and returns with a loaf of bread.

Mother Hen: Just smell this delicious homemade bread. Who will help me eat this bread?

Duck: Oh, I will!

Cat: Oh, I will!

Dog: Oh, I will!

Chorus sings "I Will."

Mother Hen: Oh no you won't! You did not help me plant the wheat or bake this bread. Come my little chicks and you can share this bread with me.

Peeping chicks enter as Chorus sings "This Was the Story."

This is the Story

words and music by S. Kay Gandy
arranged by Wiley McLary

This is the sto - -ry of the Lit - -tle Red Hen, she did - not get a help--ing hand from

an - -y of her friends. She worked all day and

did not play un - -til her work was done.

Not like the duck, the cat or the dog hav--ing so much fun.

2017

2

Not I Song

words and music by S. Kay Gandy

Work Song

words and music by S. Kay Gandy

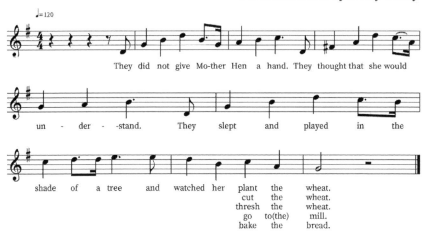

They did not give Mo-ther Hen a hand. They thought that she would

un - der - -stand. They slept and played in the

shade of a tree and watched her plant the wheat.
                                   cut the wheat.
                                   thresh the wheat.
                                   go to(the) mill.
                                   bake the bread.

I Will Song

Words and Music by S. Kay Gandy

I will said the duck, I will said the cat, I will said the dog,

I will I will, I will.

This is the Story (Reprieve)

words and music by S. Kay Gandy
arranged by Wiley McClary

This was the sto - ry of the lit - tle Red Hen, she did not get a help--ing hand from

an - -y of her friends. She worked all day and

did not play un - -til her work was done.

Not like the duck, the cat or the dog, hav--ing so much fun.

2017

Appendix B

Appendix C
Cinderella Story Comparison Chart

Book Title	Persecuted Hero/ Heroine	Mean Relatives	Magic Help	Type of Shoe	Party or Festival	Cultural Differences

Appendix D

Main Street Template for Architecture[1]

Town Name:

Building	Architectural Style	Visual Characteristics	Building Width	Visible Dates	Function

NOTE

1. Developed by Darrell P. Kruger and S. Kay Gandy for the Main Street Institutes sponsored by the Louisiana Geography Education Alliance.

Appendix E

Main Street Template for Courthouse Square[1]

Town_____

Main Street Name_____

Length_____ Width_____

Railroad Influence yes_____ no_____

Population_____

Date Established_____

Relationship of courthouse square to CBD

1. Center of CBD (May be incomplete)
2. Adjacent to CBD
3. Removed from CBD (or no CBD)

Structures on the square

1. Courthouse only major structure
2. Additional building on square

143

Courthouse location at square

1. Centered and/or setback
2. Modest setback
3. Little or no setback

Setting of courthouse square

1. Parklike setting, lawn, or trees
2. Modest parklike setting
3. Parking lots and street only

Monuments and memorials on the square

Yes_____

No_____

NOTE

1. Darrell P. Kruger and S. Kay Gandy, "Main Street in the Curriculum: A Fifteen Town Louisiana Case-Study," *Journal of Geography* 105, no. 2 (2006): 73–86.

Appendix F

Main Street Template for Building Use[1]

Town_____

Building	Information from Tenants	Information from Historical/ Aerial Photograph	Current Land Use	Sanborn Map Land Use

NOTE

1. Kruger and Gandy, "Main Street in the Curriculum," 73–86.

Appendix G

Table for Using the FILM Strategy

Iconography	Function	Importance	Location	Meaning

Appendix H

Amish Friendship Bread Recipe

STARTER FOR AMISH FRIENDSHIP BREAD

Instructions: Use a wooden spoon. Do not refrigerate. Use plain, not self-rising, flour.

Day 1: Mix together well: one cup flour, one cup sugar, and one cup milk.

Days 2, 3, 4: Stir mixture with wooden spoon. Place in a glass bowl. Cover with a dark-colored dishcloth and push to the back of your counter. Less light allows the bread to ferment easier.

Day 5: Add one cup flour, one cup sugar, one cup milk.

Day 6, 7, 8, 9: Stir back down and keep covered.

Day 10: Add one cup flour, one cup sugar, one cup milk. Divide mixture into three containers to give to friends.

AMISH FRIENDSHIP BREAD

Day 1: Do nothing.

Day 2, 3, 4, 5: Mush (knead, mash) bag of starter.

Day 6: Add one cup flour, one cup sugar, one cup milk. Mush (knead, mash) bag.

Day 7, 8, 9: Mush (knead, mash) bag and let air out.

Day 10: Add one cup flour, one cup sugar, one cup milk. Mush (knead, mash) bag, then pour four one cup starters into four Ziplock (large) bags. Give to friends.

Using what is left, in a big bowl add one cup cooking oil, half cup milk, three eggs, one teaspoon vanilla.

In a separate bowl add half teaspoon salt, one cup sugar, one teaspoon cinnamon, one cup chopped pecans, two cups flour, one-and-a-half teaspoons baking powder, half teaspoon baking soda, one large box vanilla instant pudding.

Mix well, then mix both bowls together. Use two well-greased bread pans coated with a cinnamon-sugar mixture instead of flour. Pour mixture into pans and bake at 325 degree for 45 minutes to 1 hour. You can freeze bread after baking.

Appendix I

Johnny Cake Recipe[1]

Tools: heavy twelve-inch frying pan, metal spatula, measuring cups, and spoons

Ingredients: one cup yellow cornmeal, half teaspoon salt, one cup boiling water, half cup milk

Steps:

1. Mix the cornmeal and salt.
2. Add the boiling water, stirring until smooth.
3. Add the milk; stir well.
4. Grease a heavy, twelve-inch frying pan. Set over medium-low heat.
5. Drop a tablespoonful of the batter onto the pan. Cook until golden, about five minutes.
6. Turn the cakes carefully with a metal spatula. Cook the other side for five minutes.
7. Serve the first cakes hot with butter and maple syrup while you cook the rest of the batter. Makes twelve to fifteen cakes.

NOTE

1. Lucille Recht Penner, *The Colonial Cookbook* (New York: Hastings House, 1983): 92.

Bibliography

Anderson, Derek. "Outliers: Elementary Teachers Who Actually Teach Social Studies." *The Social Studies* 105, no. 2 (2004): 91–100, DOI: 10.1080/00377996. 2013.850055.

Armstrong, Edward G. and Paul L. Greider. "The Presentation of Identity in the Work Songs of Johnny Cash." *Popular Music and Society* 36, no. 2 (2013): 216–233.

Barton, Keith C. "A Picture's Worth: Analyzing Historical Photographs in the Elementary Grades." *Social Education* 65, no. 5 (2001): 278–283.

Britt, Judy and Mandi Howe. "Developing a Vision for the Common Core Classroom: What Does Elementary Social Studies Look Like?" *The Social Studies* 105, no. 3 (2014): 158–163, doi: 10.1080/00377996.2013.866930.

Brownet, Tristi. "Social Capital and Participation: The Role of Community Arts Festivals for Generating Well-being." *Journal of Applied Arts & Health* 9, no. 1 (2018): 71–84.

Burkowski, John Jr. and Xose Manuel Alvarino, "Teaching Social Studies Through Film," The Education Fund, accessed at file:///C:/Users/stp16282/Downloads/Teaching%20Social%20Studies%20Through%20Film%20(2009).pdf.

Cooper, Elizabeth. "Something to Sink Their Teeth Into: Teaching Culture Through Food." *Transformations* 23, no. 2 (2013): 92–105,183.

Derrett, Ros. "Making Sense of How Festivals Demonstrate a Community's Sense of Place." *Event Management* 8, no. 1 (2003): 49–58.

DiDomenico, James. "Effective Integration of Music in the Elementary School Classroom." *i.e.: inquiry in education* 9, no. 2, art. 4 (2017). Accessed at https://digitalcommons.nl.edu/ie/vol9/iss2/4

Eulie, Joseph. "Creating Interest and Developing Understanding in the Social Studies through Cartoons." *Peabody Journal of Education* 46, no. 5 (1969): 288–290.

153

Evans, Michael D. "Using Classroom Debates as a Learning Tool." *Social Education* 57, no. 7 (1993): 370.

Faichney, Gavin. "Signs of the Times: Inquiry with Memorial Plaques." *Social Studies and the Young Learner* 13, no. 4 (2001): 22–24.

Filipovitch, Anthony J. and Talip Ozturk. "Teaching the Social Studies through Your Local Community." *Social Education* 76, no. 2 (2012). 85–87.

Gallavan, Nancy P., Angela Webster-Smith and Sheila S. Dean. "Connecting Content, Context, and Communication in a Sixth-Grade Social Studies Class through Political Cartoons," *The Social Studies* 103, no. 5 (2012): 188–191, doi: 10.1080/00377996.2011.605644.

Gandy, S. Kay. "Azulejos: Tile Buildings in Iquitos." *Journal of Geology & Geosciences* 3, no. 6 (2014), doi:10.4172/2329-6755.1000176.

Gandy, S. Kay. "Cajun and Creole Folktales." *Southern Social Studies Journal* 41, no. 1 (2015): 9–12.

Gandy, S. Kay. "Connections to the Past: Creating Time Detectives with Archaeology." *Social Education* 71, no. 5 (2014): 267–271.

Gandy, S. Kay. "Legacy of the American West: Indian Cowboys, Black Cowboys, and Vaqueros." *Social Education* 72, no. 4 (2008): 189–193.

Gandy, S. Kay. "Public Lands in the Elementary Curriculum," in *Stewardship of Public Lands: A Handbook for Educator.* New York: American Association of Colleges and Universities, 2010: 151–157.

Gandy, S. Kay. "Teaching Social Studies on a Shoestring Budget." *Social Education* 69, no. 2 (2005): 98–101.

Gandy, S. Kay. "Teaching the Election Process in Ten Days." *Social Education* 68, no. 5 (2004): 332–338.

Gandy, S. Kay and Cynthia Williams Resor, "Changing Technology and the U.S. Mail." *The Social Studies* 103, no 6 (2012): 226–232.

Getskow, Veronica. *Incredible Edible Geography.* Irvine, CA: Thomas Bros. Maps Educational Foundation, 1998.

Gordon, Bertram M. "Food and History." *The Social Studies* 65, no. 5, (1973): 204–207, doi: 10.1080/00220973.1943.11019347.

Groce, Eric, Rachel E. Wilson, and Lisa Poling. "Tomb It May Concern: Visit Your Local Cemetery for a Multidisciplinary (and Economical) Field Trip." *Social Studies and the Young Learner* 25, no. 3 (2013): 13–17.

Hatcher, Barbara A. "Who's in the Kitchen with Dinah? History!." *The Social Studies* 81, no. 3 (1990): 101–105.

Irshad, Humaira. "Impacts of Community Events and Festivals on Rural Places." *Agriculture and Rural Development* published by the Government of Alberta

(2011): accessed at https://www1.agric.gov.ab.ca/$Department/deptdocs.nsf/all/csi13702/$FILE/Community-events-and-festivals.pdf.

Joint Committee on Geographic Education. *Guidelines for Geographic Education: Elementary and Secondary Schools.* Washington, DC: National Council for Geographic Education and Association of American Geographers, 1984.

Kimball, Walter (ed.). *Spaces and Places: A Geography Manual for Teachers.* Washington DC: Geographic Education National Implementation Project, 1995.

Kirman, Joseph M. and Chris Jackson. "The Use of Postage Stamps to Teach Social Studies Topics." *The Social Studies* 91, no. 4 (2000): 187–190.

Kruger, Darrell P. and S. Kay Gandy. "Main Street in the Curriculum: A Fifteen Town Louisiana Case-Study." *Journal of Geography* 105, no. 2 (2006): 73–86.

LeBlanc, Heather. "Political Cartoons: 7 Ways to Step Away From the Lecture Podium & Revitalize Your Social Studies Classroom," accessed at https://www.brainyapples.com/2018/06/12/political-cartoons-in-the-social-studies-classroom/.

Libresco, Andrea. "Past and Present Imperfect: Recent History and Politics Go to the Movies." *Social Education* 81, no. 3 (2017): 148–153.

Lintner, Timothy. "Hurricanes and Tsunamis: Teaching About Natural Disasters and Civic Responsibility in Elementary Classrooms." *The Social Studies* 97, no. 3 (2006): 101–104, doi: 10.3200/TSSS.97.3.101-104.

Lintner, Timothy. "Using "Exceptional" Children's Literature to Promote Character Education in Elementary Social Studies Classrooms." *The Social Studies* 102, no. 5 (2011): 200–203, doi: 10.1080/00377996.2010.550955.

Mangram, Jeffery A. and Rachel L. Weber. "Incorporating Music into the Social Studies Classroom: A Qualitative Study of Secondary Social Studies Teachers." *The Journal of Social Studies Research* 36, no. 1 (2012): 3–21.

Marks, Melanie and Cheryl Davis. "Making the Economic Concept of Scarcity Oh-So-Sweet: An Activity for the K-12 Classroom." *The Social Studies* 97, no. 6 (2006): 239–244, doi:10.3200/TSSS.97.6.239-244.

Marino, Michael P. and Margaret S. Crocco. "Pizza: Teaching US History through Food and Place." *The Social Studies* 106, no. 4 (2015): 149–158, doi: 10.1080/00377996.2015.1020354.

Matz, Karl A. and Lori L. Pingatore. "Reel to Real: Teaching the Twentieth Century with Classic Hollywood Films." *Social Education* 69, no. 4 (2005): 189.

McCall, Ava L. "Teaching Powerful Social Studies Ideas Through Literature Circles." *The Social Studies* 101, no. 4 (2010): 152–159, doi: 10.1080/00377990903284104.

McConnell, Akila. "11 Fast Facts About the History of Pizza." ThoughtCo. (Apr. 13, 2020): accessed at https://www.thoughtco.com/history-of-pizza-1329091

McCormick, Theresa M. and Janie Hubbard, "Every Picture Tells a Story: A Study of Teaching Methods Using Historical Photographs with Elementary Students." *Journal of Social Studies Research* 35, no. 1 (2011): 80–94.

Niland, Amanda. "Musical Stories: Strategies for Integrating Literature and Music for Young Children." *Australian Journal of Early Childhood* 32, no. 4 (2007): 7–11

Nobles, Connie. *Adventures in Classroom Archaeology*. Baton Rouge, LA.: Division of Archaeology, 1992: 10–12.

Ostrom, Richard. "Active Learning Strategies for Using Cartoons and Internet Research Assignments in Social Studies Courses." *Social Studies Review* 43, no. 2 (2004): 61–64.

Panchyk, Richard. *Archaeology for Kids: Uncovering the Mysteries of Our Past*. Chicago: Chicago Review Press, 2003: 30.

Penner, Lucille Recht. *The Colonial Cookbook*. New York: Hastings House. 1983.

Prelutsky, Jack. *The New Kid on the Block*. New York: Greenwillow Books. 2013.

Psilaki, Efi. "Sharing Cultures through Food: Teaching in a Multicultural University Classroom." *Transformations: The Journal of Inclusive Scholarship and Pedagogy* 23, no. 2 (2012): 130–140.

Resor, Cynthia Williams. *Investigating Family, Food, and Housing Themes in Social Studies*. New York: Rowman & Littlefield, 2017: 67.

Resor, Cynthia Williams. "Food as a Theme in Social Studies Classes: Connecting Daily Life to Technology, Economy, and Culture." *The Social Studies* 101 (2010): 236–241, doi: 10.1080/00377990903284997.

Resor, Cynthia Williams. "Place-Based Education: What Is Its Place in the Social Studies Classroom?" *The Social Studies* 101, no. 5 (2010): 185–188.

Resor, Cynthia Williams. "Using Community Cookbooks as Primary Sources," *Social Education* 75, no. 1 (2011): 30–35.

Risinger, C. Frederick and Ray Heitzmann, "Using the Internet to Teach about Political Cartoons and Their Influence on U.S. Elections," *Social Education* 72, no. 6 (2008): 288–290.

Russell, William B. III. "The Art of Teaching Social Studies with Film," *Clearing House* 85, no. 4 (2012): 157, doi: 10.1080/00098655.2012.674984.

Shapiro, Laura. *Something from the Oven: Reinventing Dinner in 1950s America*. New York: Viking Press, 2004.

Sieber, Ellen. "Teaching with Objects and Photographs: Supporting and Enhancing Your Curriculum, A Guide for Teachers," Mathers Museum of World Cultures (2012):15–23, accessed at https://mathersmuseum.indiana.edu/doc/Tops.pdf.

Silverstein, Shel. *Where the Sidewalk Ends: Poems and Drawings*. New York: HarperCollins, 2014.

Singleton, Laurel R. *G is for Geography: Children's Literature and the Five Themes.* Boulder, CO: Social Science Education Consortium, 1993.

Singleton, Laurel R. and James R. Giese. "Using Online Primary Sources with Students." *The Social Studies* 90, no. 4 (1999):148–151, doi: 10.1080/00377999909602406.

Sunal, Cynthia Szymanski, Lynn Allison Kelley, Andrea K. Minear, Dennis W. Sunal. "Elementary Students Represent Classroom Democratic Citizenship Experiences via Photos." *The Journal of Social Studies Research* 35, no. 2 (2011): 191–216.

Thornton, Zita. "Buttons," *Antiques & Collecting Magazine* 106, no. 7 (2001): 26–30.

Vardell, Sylvia M. "Poetry for Social Studies: Poems, Standards, and Strategies." *Social Education* 67, no. 4 (2003): 206–211.

Summary of Activities

Chapter 1: Using Primary Sources to Teach Social Studies

#	Activity	Page #	Content Connections			
			Geography	History	Civics	Economics
1	Petitions for Citizenship	5	X	X	X	X
2	What's in Your Wallet?	6		X		X
3	Money, Money, Money	8		X	X	X
4	Stamp Your Story	9	X	X	X	X
5	The Flea Market	10		X		
6	Primary Debate	12			X	
7	Tiles and Patterns	13	X	X		
8	Can You Dig It?	14	X	X		

Chapter 2: Using Music to Teach Social Studies

#	Activity	Page #	Content Connections			
			Geography	History	Civics	Economics
9	Teaching Concepts through Music	21	X	X		
10	Music with a Message	23			X	
11	Nonlinguistic Representations	25	X	X		
12	Musical Instruments	26	X	X	X	
13	Types of Music	28		X		X
14	Storytelling with Music	29	X	X		
15	Dance	30	X	X		
16	Whistle While You Work	31		X	X	X

Chapter 3: Using Literature to Teach Social Studies

#	Activity	Page #	Geography	History	Civics	Economics
					Content Connections	
17	Geographic Book Reports	38	X			
18	Tradebook—Mama Do You Love Me?	40	X			X
19	Newspaper—It's a Revolution!	41	X	X	X	
20	Telephone Book Scavenger Hunt	43	X	X		
21	Poetry	44	X		X	
22	Folktales	46	X			
23	Origin Stories	48	X	X		
24	Literature Circles	50		X		

Chapter 4: Using Visual Media to Teach Social Studies

#	Activity	Page #	Geography	History	Civics	Economics
					Content Connections	
25	Small-Town Images	57	X	X	X	X
26	Cartoons and Comic Strips	58		X	X	
27	Comic Books	59		X	X	
28	Let's Go to the Movies	60		X	X	
29	Civic Photography	62			X	
30	Movie Issues	63	X	X	X	X

Chapter 5: Using the Environment to Teach Social Studies

#	Activity	Page #	Geography	History	Civics	Economics
					Content Connections	
31	The American Trail System	70	X	X		
32	Environmental Exercise: Reduce Your Waste	71	X		X	X
33	Postcards from the Edge: Endangered Species	73	X	X	X	
34	Superheroes of Public Land Management	75	X		X	
35	Backyard Habitats	77	X		X	
36	Legacy of the American West	80	X	X		X
37	War and Peace	82	X	X	X	X

Chapter 6: Using the Community to Teach Social Studies

#	Activity	Page #	Geography	History	Civics	Economics
					Content Connections	
38	Main Streets	87	X	X	X	X
39	Cemeteries	90	X	X		
40	Iconography and Landscape	94	X	X	X	
41	Community Festivals	96	X	X	X	X
42	U.S. Postal Service	99	X	X		

Chapter 7: Using Food to Teach Social Studies

	Activity	Page #		Content Connections		
#			Geography	History	Civics	Economics
43	Earth Models	105	X			
44	Origins of Food and Appliances	107	X	X		X
45	Food and Literature	110	X			X
46	Cooking and Recipes	112	X	X		X

Chapter 8: Using Experiential Learning to Teach Social Studies

	Activity	Page #		Content Connections		
#			Geography	History	Civics	Economics
47	Mock Trials	120			X	
48	World on a String	121	X			X
49	Take a Stand	123			X	
50	Town Simulation	124	X	X	X	X

About the Author and Illustrator

ABOUT THE AUTHOR

Dr. S. Kay Gandy was an elementary teacher of twenty-seven years in Louisiana and a university professor of seventeen years in Kentucky. She currently works with a social studies company and resides in Arkansas. Dr. Gandy is a perpetual student and has five degrees, including a Master of Science degree in geography. She is the author of *Mapping Is Elementary, My Dear*, a book of 100 activities to teach mapping skills to K–6 students. One of her passions is international education and she has created many opportunities for both faculty and students to travel abroad. She has received two Fulbright awards to South Africa and one to Senegal and has planned study abroad trips to Peru, England, and Costa Rica. She has worked extensively with teachers from China and led social studies workshops for teachers in New Zealand, South Africa, Spain, England, Chile, and Scotland.

ABOUT THE ILLUSTRATOR

Madalyn Stack is a graphic designer and illustrator from Louisville, Kentucky. She is currently studying at Western Kentucky University. Ms. Stack illustrated the book cover and cartoons for this book and *Mapping Is Elementary, My Dear* by the author.

Made in the USA
Monee, IL
21 August 2023

41383492R00096